A COMMENTARY

ON

THE BOOK OF

HEBREWS

BY JAMES NSWANA

2020 Edition
Published by

Jacobs Well Publisher's ©

A Commentary on the Book of Hebrews:
Bible Study Notes and Comments

Table of Contents

Dedication

I dedicate this book to my late immediate younger brother Erick Nswana Kamboyi who went to be with the Lord. We grew up together as though we were twin brothers and we always encouraged one another in terms of education at Solwezi Primary School by then. He very much motivated me through his enthusiasm to learn.

Acknowledgement

My first gratitude goes to the Lord God Almighty for His sustenance and grace. Every step of this journey was filled with His gracious acts of mercy. I sincerely thank my wife Edina Moleshi, my seven children, Shekainah, Tehillah, Hope, Faith, Nkisu, James, Roma and the only Granddaughter Gloria for their support and encouragement during the time of writing this book. My special gratitude goes to Apostle Dr Roma Nyakambumba and Bishop Cathrine Chiyezhi Nyakambumba who are my spiritual parents. They have discipled me and set a good foundation in my spiritual and academic life. I would like to thank Professor Nickson Banda for the great encouragement and the skill to write books. My special gratitude also goes to Professor Leonard Lupiya, Dr Ilubala Mwalye and Dr Evance Lupiya for their support to this book. I would like to thank my two friends Rev Dr Peter Lungu and Pastor Dr Greg Kwalombota for their great contribution to this book. My final appreciation goes to New Covenant Church in Mongu for their support and to Elder Festus Mwiya for proof Reading.

About the Author

Dr James Nswana is an ordained Bishop serving the Lord as overseer in New Covenant Churches International in Western Province of Zambia. He has planted 16 Churches in the Province and currently together with his Wife Edina are missionaries for over 20 years. He has served on the faculty of Logos University, Greenlight University and other Universities as Senior Lecturer. Dr Nswana James holds a PhD in Theology and Leadership. He is the author of *"Tested to be Trusted."* He is married to Edina Moleshi and God has blessed them with seven children and one granddaughter.

PREFACE

The book of Hebrews is complete with the most valuable instructions and heavenly wisdom. This book was written to show the spiritual nature of the Christian dispensation as it is contrasted with the Mosaic economy. The Old Covenant was carnal, typical, shadowy, and temporary as the New Covenant was spiritual, heavenly, and permanent. The author proves the infinite dignity of the Son of God, and illustrates his official superiority to the Prophets, angels, Moses, Joshua and to the Aaronic priesthood. He then explains the nature of the new covenant of which Christ is the Mediator and how it has superseded the old covenant. He reveals the all-sufficiency of the sacrifice of Christ and the insufficiency of all animal sacrifices which were simply types and never intended to be a real atonement for sin. The author furthermore, shows that we have access into the holiest place through the blood of Jesus and the boldness with which we may, under the guidance of our great High Priest; draw nigh to the mercy seat of God. He exhorts his original readers to hold on to the Christian profession steadfast up to the end despite all trials, afflictions, and sufferings for Christ. It is hoped that this expositions might be profitably used in the Colleges, Seminaries, Universities and devotional studies either at personal level or group level.

The manner in which this little book is to be used is that it will be studied alongside a bible in any version. When I do quote a Scripture, I generally quote the King James Version, unless otherwise indicated and sometimes I have paraphrased the passage in my own words. Since the New Testament was originally written it Greek language, most Greek terms perhaps, even a few Hebrew terms are included in this book to help the readers of this book to have a wider understanding of the author's thought. It has been the author's aim, to render the exposition plain, clear, and familiar; so as to bring it down to a level with the readers' mind, for whose benefit it is designed. However, he has endeavoured to give not only the right meaning, but help the readers have an acquaintance with the doctrines and practical instructions contained in the letter. But this should be regarded as preparatory to the study of the inspired letter, which unfold the mysteries of redeeming love, and teach so clearly the great articles of our faith, and the various duties of the Christian life.

And, finally, the author takes the liberty to recommend, that this exposition may be useful to anyone who has not carefully studied the inspired writings of the apostles of Jesus Christ. Therefore, by studying this exposition, a person will obtain a correct knowledge of the inspired epistles with more ease, than by studying an exposition written in a different form.

Bishop Dr James Nswana (PhD) August, 2020.

Abbreviations used

O.T– Old Testament
N.T – New Testament
NEB – New English Bible
NASB – New American Standard Bible
 KJV – King James Version
NKJV – New King James Version
ESV – English Standard Version
NIV – New International Version
RSV – Revised Standard Version
ASV – American Standard Version
Vs –Verse
f – the following verse
ff – the following verses

Introduction to Hebrews

1. Characteristics of the Book

The book of Hebrews is a letter which is entirely different from any other in the New Testament. It is based upon the principles of the Levitical priesthood. The priesthood of Christ is directly linked to the Old Levitical order. More than any other New Testament books 'Hebrews' require detailed explanations of the importance of the background. It speaks of Christ, the son and priest who is mediator of the new covenant. The author emphasizes on three words in his writing: better, believe and beware. The letter is a general epistle in that it was addressed to general, rather than specific groups of believers. The general outline of the book shows Jesus Superiority to everyone and everything. Much of the language used, the figures employed, and the references that are made, are only intelligible in the light of the Old Testament Scriptures, on which Judaism was based. The book insists on the finality of the Christian life, addresses itself to faith. It is one continued and sustained fervent and intense appeal to cleave to Jesus, the High Priest; to the substantial, true, and real worship. A most urgent and loving exhortation to be steadfast, patient, hopeful, in the presence of God, in the love and sympathy of the Lord Jesus, in the fellowship of the great cloud of witnesses. Another prominent characteristic, concerning which there is no need for us now to enlarge upon, is the repeated *warnings* in this Epistle *against apostasy.*The letter has given five warnings or practical exhortations which are; the sin of neglect (2:1-4);the sin of unbelief (3:7-4:13); the sin of apostasy (5:11-6:30), the sin of willful transgression (10:26-39) and the sin of obstinate refusal (12:15-29)In Hebrews 13:22 there is a striking word which defines the *character* of this letter: "And I beseech you, brethren, suffer the word *of exhortation,* for I have written a letter unto you in few words."

2. Purpose of the Letter

The letter was written to a group of 1st century Christians who were in a danger of giving up. It is very clear that the times were hard for Jewish Christians especially. Many of them were exposed to fierce persecution. They had been physically assaulted, some had been cast into prison because of their trust in Jesus, and others had been ridiculed in the public. Many of the believers had accepted all these challenges joyfully. But others had shrunk back from their earlier love and commitment to Jesus and became apostates. Some others were in dangers of Compromise. The letter appeals all these Christians to keep their faith firmly in the midst of severe test. Before he gives pastoral exhortations, the author reminds the believers of the uniqueness of Jesus Christ. The author shows that the new covenant is superior to and supplants the old covenant because it is mediated by the son, who is both priest and sacrifice. God speaks and is author of both covenants. The aim of the author is twofold: To show the non- believing Hebrew that the new covenant far supersedes the old and to lead the Hebrew believers to nature knowledge of the New Testament truth.

3. Theme

The theme of this letter is the supremacy and sufficiency of Jesus Christ as revealer and as mediator of God`s grace (1:1-4) Christ is God`s full and final revelation than in the Old Testament.

4. Authorship

The authorship of the epistle to the Hebrews has been a subject of controversy from earliest times. The earliest church could not determine the author. The letter of Hebrews shows that, the author must have had authority in the apostolic church; has been an intellectual Hebrew Christian; who knew the Torah and one who knew the spiritual condition of the Hebrew converts.

Some of those suggested to the authorship includes:

Paul

An unknown author and some say it was Paul who wrote this letter. Paul as the author has also been the official Roman Catholic view since the Council of Trent (A.D. 1545–1563). The book was commonly known as "the epistle of Paul to the Hebrews." Horne states: "the Christian church generally [attributed the book] to Saint Paul." But the author does not make any personal reference to himself in this letter. Hebrews 2:3, shows that the author of Hebrews was neither an apostle nor an eyewitness nor received special revelation directly from the risen Christ as Paul (Galatians 1:11-12; 1 Corinthians 9:1). The author aligns with those who have secondhand knowledge of the Lord, something that Paul strongly denied. The literary style is different from the other Pauline writings. Anyway, this epistle was written by an inspired believer to a persecuted suffering group of Jews somewhere in the East. The style of Hebrews, however, differs greatly from Paul's letters. For example, it includes none of Paul's Hebraisms, none of his long-involved sentences, none of his rapid changes in thought, and none of his usual way of introducing Old Testament quotations. In addition, the style of the Greek in this letter is the most elegant and pure in the New Testament, closer to Luke's writing and unlike any of Paul's letters. Perhaps the strongest argument against Pauline authorship is the considerable theological difference between Hebrews and Paul's writings.

Barnabas

Barnabas was a companion of Apostle Paul on his first missionary trip (Acts 9:27; 11:22-26; 12:25; 13:1–14:28; 15:1-41). He was a Levite (Acts 4:36) and thoroughly familiar with the priestly services. Barnabas was called "Son of Encouragement." However, because of Levite connections Tertullian (c. A.D. 160–230) and scholars of North Africa suggested Barnabas to the authorship. In spite of this strong endorsement, there is no other sufficient support for Barnabas as the author of this book.

Apollos

Apollos was an Alexandrian Barnabas and was a Jew of priestly tribe of Levi (Acts 4:36).He was Paul's companion (close friend) after Paul's conversion and in the early years of the church in Corinth (1 Corinthian 1:12; 3:4-6, 22). (Acts 13:1-4).By faith, Apollos was also a Jewish Christian who was learned with great knowledge of scriptures and he was an eloquent speaker (preacher). It was also said of Apollos that "This man was instructed in the way of the Lord; and being fervent in the spirit, he spake and taught diligently the things of the Lord, knowing only the baptism of John. And he began to speak boldly in the synagogue: whom when Aquila and Priscilla had heard, they took him unto *them,* and expounded unto him the way of God more perfectly. " For the mightily convinced the Jews, *and that* publicly, shewing by the scriptures that Jesus was Christ (Act 18:24-26, 28). Therefore, Apollos combined the eloquence of the Greek with the religious instinct of the Jew. He was a student from the great university at Alexandria, a convert to the gospel, deeply conversant with the Old Testament, gifted with eloquence; he was a strong ally of the Christian forces of his age. But he needed to know of the death, resurrection, and ascended power of Christ, and to experience the Pentecostal gift. Into all these he was led by Aquila and Priscilla. Luther proposed Apollos as the author, and many modern scholars lean in that direction because the epistle displays the kind of allegorical interpretations that were prominent in Alexandria.

Luke

According to Clement of Alexandria and Origen belief, Luke is the one that translated original writings of Apostle Paul. Parts of Hebrews are similar to the style and content of Acts, especially Stephen's speech (Acts 7:1-53), but that is the only proposed connection between Hebrews and Luke. However, this is just a speculation.

5. Audience

This epistle, like James and 1 Peter, was written to Jewish Christians. It is clearly addressed to Hebrews. The author had in mind both non- believing and believing Hebrews, who might have lived in Jerusalem or Rome (13:24). These Hebrews were conversant with temple worship. They did not fully understand that the Leviticus sacrifices were to be abrogated by the new covenant. The epistle was written at the time of transition (from old covenant temple ritual to the new covenant with its spiritual sanctuary, spiritual priest, and spiritual worship as opposed to the earthly and material ritualism. The absence of references to Gentiles in this book indicates that the readers must be Jewish Christians. They had come out of Judaism in which they were born and brought up. Now they were born again. They had accepted Jesus as their personal Saviour. In this book the Lord was speaking to these Christians and telling them to hold to the supreme priesthood and not to go back into the patterns of Judaism. In the group of Hebrews to whom this letter was written, there were non-believers who knew Jesus is the Christ and were not willing to commit themselves to Him. The author warns these people that if they know the truth of the gospel and reject it, the consequence will be terrible.

6. Date of this Letter

We cannot be absolutely certain about the date of this letter. At the time the epistle was written, priests were still offering sacrifices. This indicates that the temple was still standing, (8:4; 10:11; 13:10) before its destruction in AD 70, (10:25). It has been suggested that the epistle was written somewhere between 63 and 66 AD. But chapter10: 32-34 is considered as a reference to Neronian Persecution in AD 64. This epistle was known by clement of Rome at the end of first century. So it will be safe to assume that the book of Hebrews was written in the second half of first century.

7. Its Divisions

The first is by far the larger division, reaching from the chapter 1:1 of the letter to chapter 10:18. The second division begins Chapter 10: 19 to the end of the letter. The superiority of Christianity to Judaism is the great doctrine which the letter teaches; and loyalty in the faith and profession of that religion, is the great duty which it enjoins.

Family Tree

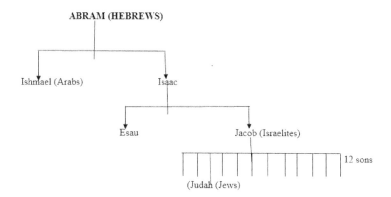

Outline of the Book

I. The supremacy of Jesus (1:1-4:13)

A. Jesus is better than Prophets (1:1-2:4)

1. The Son was appointed heir of all things (vs.2)

2. The Son is the creator of the universe (vs.2)

3. The Son is the brightness of His Glory (vs.3)

4. The Son is the express image of His person (vs.3)

5. The Son upholds all things by the word of his power (vs.3)

6. The Son sat down at the right hand of the majesty in heaven (vs.3)

B. Jesus is better than Angels (1:4-14)

1. The Son has obtained a more excellent name than angels (vs.4, 5)

2. The Son has Superior dignity than angels (vs.6)

3. The Son has Superior Nature than angels (vs.7, 9)

C. The sin of Neglect (2:1-4)

D. The humanity of Jesus (2:5-18)

1. To bringing many to glory (2:10)

2. To present to God a sanctified people (2:11)

3. To destroy him that had the power of death (2:14)

E. Jesus is better than Moses (3:1-6)

F. The Sin of Unbelief (3:7-19)

G. Jesus is better than Joshua (Hebrews 4:1-13)

1. The better rest (4:3-14)

2. The three phases of "rest"

3. The Sabbath day as a shadow

4. The Redemption Rest For God's People

5. God's word is powerful (4:12, 13)

II. The Superiority of Jesus' Priesthood (4:14-8:6)

A. Jesus is better than Aaron

B. Qualifications for a Priest (5:1-4)

1. He was to be a man

2. He was called of God.

3. He was to be sympathetic

C. Jesus the Perfect High Priest (5:5-10)

1. Jesus had to be a man

 2. Jesus was Sympathetic with men

3. Jesus offered Sacrifice for men

4. Jesus was appointed by God

D. The Sin of Apostasy (5:11-6:20)

1. Failing to mature (5:12-14)

2. Principles of the Doctrine of Christ (6:1-3)

3. Apostasy: Rejecting Christ (6:4-6)

4. The Basis for our Steadfastness (6:13-20)

E. Jesus the Priest of Melchizedek's Order (7:1-28-8:6)

1. The facts of Melchizedek's significance (7:1-10)

2. The Change of priesthood (7:11-19)

3. Jesus Christ the Priest Forever (7:20-28)

4. Our High Priest Ministers in Heaven (8:1-6)

III. The Superiority of the New Covenant (8:7-10:18)

A. Old Covenant to be replaced by the new (8:7-13)

B. The Symbolic Sanctuary (9:1-10)

1. Articles of the tabernacle (9:1-5)

2. Sacrifices and rituals in the tabernacle (9:6-10)

C. Jesus' sacrifice compared to animal sacrifices (9:11-15)

D. The shedding of blood (9:16-23)

E. The better sacrifice offered only once (9:24-28)

F. The insufficiency of animal sacrifices (10:1-4)

G. God's eternal will (10:5-10)

H. Jesus the Perfect Sacrifice (10:11-18)

IV. Applications to Faithfulness (10:19-13:25)

A. Drawing Near to God (10:19-39)

1. Holding Fast and Assembling with the Saints (10:19-25)

2. Avoiding willful sin (10:26-31)

3. The past sacrifices and sufferings (10:32-39)

B. Old Testament examples of faithfulness (chapter 11)

1. Faith as defined by Hebrew (11:1-3)

2. The more excellent Sacrifice (11:4)

3. Faith is necessary to please God (11:5-6)

4. Heir of the Righteousness by Faith (11:7)

5. The Doctrine of Faith (11:8-12)

6. The Perseverance of Faith (11:13-16)

7. The Faith of Abraham in Sacrificing Isaac (11:17-19)

8. The Faith of Isaac and Jacob (11:20-22)

9. The Faith of Moses' parents (11:23-26)

10. The Faith of Moses (11:27-29)

11. Other Heroes of Faith (11:32-34)

12. The Heroes of Faith Tested in Hardships (11:35-40)

C. Things that encourage faithfulness (chapter 12)

1. Running the Race (12:1-4)

2. The Discipline of God (12:5-11)

Hebrews 1

II. The supremacy of Jesus (1:1-4:13)

A. Jesus is better than Prophets (1:1-2:4)

The letter to Hebrews begins by stating the greatest fact of the Christian revelation. The letter does not begin with introductory greeting of any kind, but launches immediately into its theme. Jesus is the channel of creation, providence and redemption. He is the far-traveled ray of Deity; but not one among many equals, for of Him alone could it be said that His nature was co-extensive with God's. God has spoken to man through his word in the Bible and through Jesus; His Son. He is on the throne, not merely because of His original nature, but as the reward of His obedience unto death, Philippians 2:9. In Christ, God has closed the communication gap of all time, which exists between a sinless God and sinful mankind. The Son is better than prophets. Let us now have a look at the four contrasts between the Old Covenant and New Covenant in this manner; firstly, there are two different points of time given namely,

God spoke in *"time past,"* (13:1) which is all the time before the birth of Christ and in this "time past" all things through the prophets were pointing to Jesus

Christ. These *"last days"* (13:1) are the time of the fulfillment of all the promises found in the Old Covenant. Jesus is the supreme revelation of God Himself that He has given us in these last days. These last days began with the birth of Jesus Christ unto his death on the Cross of Calvary. This death ushered in a new dispensation called the new covenant. Secondly, there were fragmentary revelations and a final revelation described as, God spoke *"at Sundry times"* (13:1) in many parts and through many prophets. God spoke in diverse manners, in various methods. God spoke and revealed Himself to His People in types, visions, dreams, ceremonies, and symbols though the prophets. These *"last days"* (13:2) expresses that there is no more a progress in revelation; God is not speaking in various methods as in time past, but God has spoken by His Son who is the final revelation of Himself to people and thirdly, there are two parties that are addressed namely, God spoke in times past unto the *"fathers"* (13:2) like Abraham, Isaac and Jacob. Abraham was father of the Hebrews but by faith, he is the father of all those that believe in Christ Jesus. But in these last days, God has spoken unto *"us"* (13:2).Fourthly, there are two different mouth pieces through whom God spoke, which are "prophets" like Moses, David, Isaiah, David, John the Baptist etc., but in these last days, God has spoken by "His Son". 1 Peter 1:2 says, "Who by him do believe in God that raised him up from the dead and gave him glory; that your faith and hope might be in God." We do not fear God with the fear of the slave or felon, but with the fear of the love that cannot endure the thought of giving pain to the loving and loved. Who can think of returning to Egypt, when such a Passover lamb has redeemed us! Our redemption was not an after-thought with God but is part of an eternal plan which He prepared. The prophets were just the organ of Prophecy while the Son is the originator and object of prophecy. The prophets gave voice but the Son is the Word that Apostle John describes him as the word that was in the beginning, the word that was with God and the word which was God. He continued to say that all things were made by him; and without him was not anything made that was made. In him was life; and the life was the light of men. And the light shineth in darkness; and the darkness comprehended it not. (John 1:1-5)

Therefore, Jesus stands to be better than the prophets in that;

1. The Son was appointed heir of all things (vs.2)

As the only Son, Jesus inherits everything the Father possesses. What a wonder that those who were once in ignorance can dwell in the Eternal Light, through the Eternal Love that Jesus showed us on the Cross. It is not enough to receive the forgiveness of sins, but we must be conformed to the image of the Son, who is Himself the image of the invisible Father, the pre-eminence of Jesus in creation.

2. The Son is the creator of the universe (vs.2)

In Colossians 1:16 the word Universe or World here is "age." Which is the earth and its history throughout the ages. He is the head of His Church, in resurrection, and in the reconciliation and restoration of the saints.

3. The Son is the brightness of His Glory (vs.3)

Brightness here means reflection. In Greek, the word "brightness" [apaugasma] can describe a reflection of what is external or of what is internal. With Jesus, both are true, for his brightness perfectly reveals God's glory. His brightness is derived from the Father, even though he himself is the light. The son causes the brightness of the father to shine forth. Just as the moon receives its light from the sun and reflects the light beams to the earth, the Son's brightness is the extension of God's glory. What the pillar of cloud and fire was to Israel in the wilderness is the same way Jesus is to His Church (Exodus13:21; Numbers 9:15-23). The fire in the cloud was prophetic of His deity enshrined in His humanity. It was this consciousness of the union of the divine and human that enabled our Lord to speak as He did of Himself. He bare record of Himself, because He could say nothing less, and knew whence He came and whither

He went; and the miracles which He wrought in union with the Spirit of God ratified His witness (John 8:12).Jesus preexisted and evidently there was a process of self-limitation. The word *"Dwelt"* among his *means* that he*"tabernacled"*among us. As the Shekinah light was veiled by the curtain of the Tabernacle, so the divine essence in Jesus was veiled by His humanity, though it shone out on the mountain of transfiguration (Seen with Moses and Elijah). Jesus was full of *grace,* the unmerited love of God; full of *truth,* coming to bear witness to it; full of *glory,* that of the only begotten Son. There are many sons, but only one Son. (John 1:14)

4. The Son is the express image of His person (vs.3)

God himself stamped upon his Son the divine imprint of His being. The word translated as *"express image"* refers to minted coins that bear the image of a Sovereign or president. It is a precise reproduction of the original, though both an imprint is the same as the stamp that makes the impression though they both exist separately. The Son bears the exact imprint of the Father's being (glory) from eternity (John 14:9-11).

The theme in Hebrews 1:3 is similar to that which Paul develops in Colossians 1:15-18. Mark the steps that are describing Jesus in Philippians 2:6-11; He was in the form of God, that is, as much God as He was afterward a servant; *being in the form of God... took the form of a servant*. He did not grasp equality with God, for it was already His. He emptied Himself that is, refused to avail Himself of the use of His divine attributes, that He might teach the meaning of absolute dependence on the Father. He obeyed as a servant the laws which had their source in Him. He became man a humble man, a dying man, a crucified man. He lay in the grave. But the meaning of His descent was that of His ascent, and to all His illustrious names is now added that of *Jesus-Savior*. This must be our model. This mind must be in us. In proportion as we become humbled and crucified, we, in our small measure, shall attain the power of blessing and saving men. Apostle Paul in I Timothy 3:16 also describes him as, God who manifested in the flesh, justified in the Spirit, seen of angels, preached unto the Gentiles, believed on in the world and was received up into glory.

5. The Son upholds all things by the word of his power (vs.3)

This phrase indicates a sequence in the redemptive deeds of Christ. The word *"upholding"* means *carrying*. The Son carries "all things: to bring them to their destined end. He upholds all things by His powerful word. "And he is before all things, and by him all things consist" (Col 1:17).Thereafter, he ascended to heaven and took his rightful place of honor next to God the

Father. Christ was both the High priest and the sacrifice when he offered himself for the purification of the sins of his people. We are in Him so far as justification is concerned-that is our standing; and He is in us for sanctification-that is the source of a holy and useful life. The condition of a blessed life is the conscious maintenance of this oneness.

The source of all we are, and have, and hope to be, so far as salvation is concerned, is the will of God for us; but the stream flows to us through our Lord, and the end to which all things are moving is the summing-up of all in Christ. As He was the Alpha, so He will be the Omega. The reiteration of the prepositions *in* and *with* emphasizes our close identification with our Savior. In union with Him we have once and forever put away the sins of the flesh, have lain in His grave, have passed to the heaven side of death, and are living on earth in acceptance of God. Jesus won victory and we who have believed in him do share its fruits. Yet faith must apprehend and affirm these blessings. God has given us every provision for a godly life, through the knowledge of Jesus, but that we must avail ourselves of it. The promises are great and precious, but we must appropriate and absorb them, if we are through them to partake of the divine nature. Our redemption has been secured by our Savior (Ephesians 1:7; Colossians 1:14; 2 Peter 1:9).

6. The Son sat down at the right hand of the majesty in heaven (vs.3)

The expression *sat down at the right hand* is symbolic not literal. It signifies a privilege granted to a highly honored person. In typical Hebraic style, to perhaps to avoid offending any of his Jewish readers, the author refers to God as the majesty in heaven of course, elsewhere in the letter he freely uses God`s name. "Wherefore God also hath highly exalted him, and given him a name which is above every name: That at the name of Jesus every knee should bow, of *things* in heaven, and *things* in earth, and *things* under the earth; And *that* every tongue should confess that Jesus Christ *is* Lord, to the glory of God the Father. (Philippians 2:9-11). "Who *is* he that condemneth? *It is* Christ that died, yea rather, that is risen again, who is even at the right hand of God, who also maketh intercession for us." (Romans 8:34), "If ye then be risen with Christ, seek those things which are above, where Christ sitteth on the right hand of God." (Colossians 3:1). We belong to the world on the threshold of which Jesus said, *"Touch me not, for I am not yet ascended."* We must guard against the defiling touch of the world, of sin, and of the old self-life. We stand between two worlds, each solicits us: let us yield to the influences that pull us upward, and not to those that anchor us to this sinful and vain world. Some of the Jewish Christians in the first century had given up their faith as they no longer recognized the deity of Christ and his equality with God. The author of this letter first of all tries to expound and exalt God's Son. (Colossians 1:15-20)

B. Jesus is better than Angels (1:4-14)

Most Jews esteemed the angels as highest being next to God and hence some even believed that angels acted as God's senate or council and that He did nothing without consulting them. Many believed that the old covenant was brought to them from God by angel. They considered angels as mediators and so they were very much exalted. The author of the book of Hebrews portrays Jesus as better than angels in the following different ways;

1. The Son has obtained a more excellent name than angels (vs.4, 5)

Jesus Christ is better than angels because he has an *"excellent name"* which is "Son of God." The angels had always been ministers and messengers. For unto which of the angels said he at any time, Thou art my Son, this day have I begotten thee? And again, I will be to him a Father, and he shall be to me a Son? The Lord Jesus Christ is the Son of God. The angels are created servants. To act as messengers was the function of angels. Christ has a name superior to that of angels.

2. The Son has Superior dignity than angels (vs.6)

And again, when he bringeth in the first begotten into the world, he saith, and let all the angels of God worship him. The angels were worshippers, but He is the one they worship. At His birth they united in worship and did so because God has asked them to do. "Let the angels of God worship Him" Psalm 97:7 says, "worship Him all his angels". It is the angel's task to exalt the Son.

3. The Son has Superior Nature than angels (vs.7, 9)

Since Christ created the angels, He is superior to them for they are His created servants, His winds and flame of God's purposes. And of the angels he saith, who maketh his angels spirits, and his ministers a flame of fire. But unto the Son *he saith,* Thy throne, O God, *is* forever and ever: a sceptre of righteousness *is* the sceptre of thy kingdom. But Christ is having incomparable deity and is in contrast to the angels. Jesus is eternal God. The title Son is not a mere name showing his work on earth. It defines a relationship, which is of eternal quality. Presenting Christ's duty, the author wanted to warn the Hebrew Christians that to turn their back on Christ was to forsake God. In Hebrew 1: 10-12, the Holy Spirit reveals that Christ is better than the angels because He exists eternally. If Jesus was in the beginning before creation, He must have existed before the beginning and so he is without beginning. Psalm 102:25-27, the sixth quotation, also referred to Messiah. The Son is also Creator (cf. v. 2). This verse looks back to the past. "Lord" means "Master" Gr. [kurie], and refers to God in the passage the author quoted. No angel has ever been promised a place at God's right hand. Only the Son will sit there. The destiny of Jesus Christ is that at last everything in the universe will be subject to him. Jesus' destiny is eternal reign over the new heavens and the new earth. But the angel's destiny is to serve forever those who are heirs of salvation. The word "salvation" Gr. [soteria] occurs seven times in Hebrews, more than in any other book of the New Testament.[1]

---

[1] For a study of salvation in Hebrews, see Brenda B. Colijn, "'Let Us Approach': Soteriology
in the Epistle to the Hebrews," Journal of the Evangelical Theological Society 39:4
(December 1996):571-86.

Hebrews 2

C. The sin of Neglect (2:1-4)

After the Author showed that Jesus is superior to angels, he concludes by saying *"therefore"* (vs.1) we should not drift away from the truths we have heard from Jesus (1 Corinthians 10:12; Galatians 5:4). Here is the first of many warnings in Hebrews urging these Jewish Christians to not leave the true gospel to go into the error of returning to the Old Covenant and its ordinances. These Jewish Christians were being urged, pressured, and persecuted so that they can return to Judaism. The letter repeatedly makes application showing they should continue in the gospel because it is superior to the Old Covenant. (vs.2) The sin of *neglect* is equivalent to *reject*. Some of them decided to even quit serving God whereas they had been zealous and devoted. Apostasy is generally a gradual, slow change well described as "drifting." We begin with neglecting, disobeying, or changing some seemingly small things. Eventually, we neglect or change something more, never really intending to give up serving God. To avoid this drifting we must indeed give earnest heed to the things we have heard. These people knew the truth that they had "heard" (vs.3) He also that is slothful in his work is brother to him that is a great waster (Proverbs 18:9). The effect of deliberate rebellion and the effect of neglect are ultimately the same: God's work is not done. Both are worthy of Divine punishment. If sin was punished under the Old Testament, why should we think sins will not be punished under the New Testament?

The apostles and prophets who had God's true message could do miracles to "bear witness" (vs.4) that the message they preached was from God. The different terms for miraculous powers used here do not so much refer to different kinds of powers as they simply emphasize different effects accomplished by those powers. "Sign" emphasizes the witness or confirming nature of the events to prove they were from God. "Wonder" emphasizes the marvelous impression made on people by the events. "Miracle" indicates the nature of the events were such they could only come from God. They were "gifts of the Spirit" in that the Holy Spirit gave men the power to do these works. (1 Corinthians 12-14)

D. The Humanity of Jesus Christ (2:5-18)

In chapter one, we saw "the superiority of the Son over the angels." He is seen as the Son of God. In chapter two we see "the humiliation of the Son below angels." He is seen as the Son of Man. He is here depicted as the suffering messiah not as the reigning messiah.

The object of His incarnation was His death: in this passage the word death occurs five times. *"For the suffering of death,"*(vs. 9) Forasmuch then as the children are partakers of flesh and blood, he also himself likewise took part of the same; that *through death* he might destroy him that had the power of death, that is, the devil; (vs. 14).*"Fear of death"* And deliver them who through *fear of death* were all their lifetime subject to bondage. (2:15). Death is the penalty of sin and by His death the penalty of sin has been paid for. He became a sinless ransom for many.

Not only was Jesus "made a little lower than angels for the suffering of death" but he was also crowned with glory and honor." (Philippians1: 4) The first Adam was disobedient unto death, bringing people to ruin yet the last Adam was obedient unto death, bringing people to life. The main purpose of his death was mainly;

1. To bringing many to glory (2:10)

The Son is seen here as the captain of salvation. The word "captain" means leader or author. It means *file-leader*. The Church follows its Leader, Jesus Christ, in single file through this world, the cross and the grave, to the glory. But notice that God Himself is engaged in bringing us through; and He cannot lose one. He is made perfect through suffering.

The word "perfect" could be translated "mature" or equipped" (1 Timothy 3:16).

2. To present to God a sanctified people (2:11)

The phrase "he that sactifieth" refers to the Lord Christ Jesus. "They that are sanctified" refers to the saints. In

Hebrew "sanctification" is associated with Christ never with the Holy Spirit. It refers to position not to condition and its meaning is consecration, not purification. Sanctification means to separate. (Heb 2:11; 9:13; 10:10; 14: 29; 13:12; Exodus 11:7) The sanctifier and the sanctified "are all of one" literally, "out of one". In order for Jesus to sanctify us, He had to be "one" with us: He had to share our nature.

He had to be made lower than the angels (verse 9) and partake of flesh and blood (vs. 14). He and we have the same nature because we have the same Father. Jesus took our nature as a human when God sent Him to earth. So we are of one nature having one Father.

The thought is that the Lord and the saints are all out of one Source. The Greek word for brother [adelphos] means "from the same womb" meaning that both of them are from one source and that source is God. Joseph, who had been exalted to a place of honour and dignity, was not ashamed to call his brothers "brethren." Since He partook of our nature, He willingly refers to those He has sanctified as His "brethren." The author quotes Psalms 22:22 in which David speaks of declaring God's name to his brethren, singing praise to God in the midst of the congregation. They were "all of one." Elevation did not alter Revelation. (John 1:11, 2:13; 8:17; Isaiah 7:3, Isaiah 8:3). Isaiah`s name means "Jehovah Saviour" and these names were symbols of victory.

3. To destroy him that had the power of death (2:14)

Our Elder Brother has encountered our foes, and won deliverance for all who believe. Death remains, but its teeth are drawn and its power is annulled. Since we, the "children" (verse 13), have flesh and blood, and since Jesus wanted to defeat the power of death, He had to share in flesh and blood. He defeated death by dying and then being raised from the dead (1 Corinthians 15:20-27, 54-57; 2 Timothy 1:10; Revelation 1:17, 18). This proved that God has superior power even over death. As God, Jesus could never die. But in order to save man, He had to die. This required Him to take the form of man.

The author brings the following points of Jesus` human nature:

a)   He was lower than the angels and was concerned with men not angel in his mission (2: 9,16)

b)   He shared flesh and blood like his brothers (2: 14)

c)   While in the flesh he was subject to temptation.

d)   He prayed and offered supplication with loud cries and tears (5:7)

e)   He learnt obedience through suffering death and he is made perfect through the same (2:10)

f)   He considered death as an inevitable part of his mission (2:9, 19)

Christ's offering himself as a willing sacrifice is specially connected with the human body of Jesus. In this letter the concepts of Jesus divine Sonship and his perfect humanity goes parallel. The author presents the Son who reflects God's glory and the man who can be tempted, very clearly and together.

To make propitiation for us and become our merciful High Priest (2:17, 18)

Another reason why He became human was so that He could be our faithful and merciful High Priest. Jesus' priesthood will be discussed at length later (see references listed under 3:1). Jesus was not just the sacrifice but was also the priest who offered the sacrifice to God on behalf of men. This also required Jesus to become a man so that He could properly have mercy on us and aid us. To make propitiation means to appease. Note that we do not appease God. Of ourselves, nothing we could do could atone for our sins. But God made the propitiation through sending Jesus as our sacrifice. Through the suffering and death of Jesus, He demonstrated to us that He does understand our problems and can properly present our case to his Father. This was proof to Hebrew Christians why they should appreciate Jesus, His provisions and His plan for humanity.

This is a clear indication that they should serve Him, not neglect Him.

Hebrews 3

E. Jesus is better than Moses (3:1-6)

"Both Jesus and Moses were faithful to God in fulfilling their duties" (3:1, 2)

The author has stated that Jesus is greater than prophets (1:1-3), and He is greater than angels (1:4-2:4). This is reason why the Hebrews should continue to follow Him, not return to the Old Testament. Now the author furthermore exalts Jesus in the eyes of these Hebrews by comparing Jesus to Moses and he says Jesus is greater than Moses. The phrase "holy brethren" is not used by the apostle to indicate relationship of race, as brethren in the Hebrew race, but the relationship of believers in Christ (Hebrews 2:11, 17).

The word "holy" here means "set apart for God" and does not have particular reference to a holy work, but to a position in **salvation**- "sanctified in Christ Jesus."[2] It is

---

[2] He calls them "holy brethren." Stuart takes holy as meaning "consecrated, devoted, i.e. to Christ, set apart as Christians." The people of Israel were called holy in the same sense, not because they were spiritually holy, but because they were set apart and adopted as God's people. The word saint, at the commencement of Paul's Epistles, means the same thing.

the position of the believers secured by the redemptive work of Christ on the cross (Hebrews 2:11; Hebrews 10:10, 14) because of this position and privilege, the Holy Spirit enables us to walk in holiness. The Christian Hebrews were no longer partakers of the earthly calling or inheritance promised to Abram, Isaac and Jacob but are partakes of the heavenly calling. (Romans 11:2; Zech 12:10).These individual Hebrews were "partakers" is translated "partakers" or "associates" of the same calling.The Christians' "calling" [klensis] refers to the process by which we were instructed how to become Christians. Therefore, to be partakers of the "calling" simply means to be Christians. Moses in type represents the apostleship of Christ. Moses was a great leader of the Hebrew nation, and the author does not speak of the failures of Moses. Both the Son and Moses are called to lead. Moses led the Israelites from the bondage under pharaoh to the Promised Land yet Jesus led all people of different races and nations from the bondage of the devil to eternal life. (2:14-15).

"Jesus has more glory than Moses" (3:3, 4)

The Son is worthy of more glory than a servant. Moses so ruled the Church, which he was still a part and member of it; but Christ being the builder, is superior to the whole building. Moses while ruling others, also ruled himself, as he was a servant; but Christ being a Son possesses supreme power.The Son of God was the builder of the house of Israel. The Son is the builder and

Moses is a member in the house. House here is a metaphor used in Scripture referring to the Church as the house of God. (1Timothy 3:15) And as it is composed of the faithful, each of them is called a living stone. (1 Peter 2:5) They are also sometimes called the vessels with which the house is furnished. (2 Timothy 2:20) Moses was not the builder and founder of the house of Israel. In fact the greater the house is, the more it shows how great the maker is. But Jesus is the maker of the *Universe*. See how great that makes Him? Surely He is greater than Moses, who, as a man, was simply part of what the Creator made. There is then no one so eminent that he is not a member, and included in the universal body. God being the builder, alone is to be set above his own work; but God dwells in Christ, so that whatever is said of God is applicable to him. If it be again objected and said that Moses was no less a master builder than Paul who gloried in this title: to this I reply that this name is applied to prophets and teachers but not with strict correctness; for they are only the instruments and indeed dead instruments, except the Lord from heaven gives efficacy to what they do; and then they so labor in building the Church, that they themselves form a part of the structure; but the case is wholly different as to Christ, for he ever builds up the Church by the power of his own Spirit.

Moses was a servant in the house, but Jesus is a Son over the house. (3:5, 6)

Moses was faithful in the house as a servant but Christ as Son over the house is faithful. The words, *in his entire house,* may be applied to Moses; but I prefer to apply them to Christ, as he may be said to be faithful to his Father in ruling his whole house. Moses' work pointed forward to future glories and it was a testimony of something to come. His work was not the final product, but just a temporary step on the path to the goal that God was preparing. Jesus is the one who brought the final product and He Himself was the central figure. For the word *hope* I take for faith; and indeed hope is nothing else but the constancy of faith. He mentions *confidence* and *rejoicing,* or glorying, in order to express more fully the power of faith.[3]

---

[3] It is better for "hope" here to be retained in its proper meaning; for in verse 12 the defect of it is traced to unbelief. Were the words "confidence" and "rejoicing" rendered adjectivally, the meaning would be more evident, — "If we hold firm our confident and joyful hope to the end." So we may render a similar form of expression in verse 13, "through deceitful sin," as "newness of life" in Romans 6:4, means "new life." The most common practice is to render the genitive in such instances as an adjective, but this is not always the case. Hope is "confident" or assured, while it rests on the word of God, and is "joyful" while it anticipates the glory and happiness of the heavenly kingdom. But Beza and Doddridge take words apart, "freedom of profession and boasting of hope," or according to Beza, "the hope of which we boast." Macknight renders them "the boldness and the glorifying of the hope." The secondary meaning of the word παρρησία is confidence, and of καύχημα, joy or rejoicing, and the most suitable here, as it comports better with holding fast, or firm.

The second difference is, that to Moses was committed a doctrine to which he, in common with others, was to submit; but Christ, though he put on the form of a servant, is yet Master and Lord, to whom all ought to be subject; for, as we found in chap. 1:2, he the heir of all things.

F. The Sin of Unbelief (3:7-19)

The author has introduced the need for holding fast our confidence and our hope firm to the end (vs. 6). He now reminds the Hebrews of some history about their fathers in the wilderness who did not hold fast to God's will for them but persistently went into error.

"As in the provocation," (vs.7) *It* was for two reasons necessary for them to be reminded of the disobedience of their fathers; for as they were foolishly inflated on account of the glory of their race, they often imitated the vices of their fathers as though they were virtues, and defended themselves by their examples; and further, when they heard that their fathers were so disobedient to God, they were thus more fully taught that this admonition was not superfluous. As both these reasons existed even in the Apostle's time, he readily accommodated to his own purpose what had been formerly said by David, in order that those whom he addressed might not imitate their fathers too much.

For that reason God punished them (Read Psalm 95:7-11).The people who failed to enter Canaan are those who heard the word of God's promise concerning the land and they refused to believe what God had promised. (Exodus 17:1-7) Israel's hardness of heart when there was no water at Rephidim and they murmured against Moses. The word "err" means to wonder," (Isaiah 29:24 and 35:8). Israel was prone to be led astray.

"Take heed, brethren," (3:12, 13) For as by nature we are inclined to evil, we have need of various helps to retain us in the fear of God. Unless our faith be now and then raised up, it will lie prostrate; unless it be warmed, it will be frozen; unless it be roused, it will grow torpid. Still men disbelieve and disobey; still they doubt that God is able; still they err in their hearts and therefore fail to understand with their heads; still they wander to and fro, with weary souls and restless feet. The warning then is to *beware*. Just as an evil heart of unbelief developed in their ancestors resulting in departure or apostasy from God, so the same thing could happen to those to whom the epistle is addressed (and to us). To go back to the Old Testament is to depart from God. We cannot serve God successfully by claiming to follow Old Testament teaching. Sin does not seem so evil, and the gospel loses its attraction. Hearts are not touched by the gospel appeal. This process is called "hardening" of the heart or searing the conscience (1 Timothy 4:2; Matthew 13:13-15). But if they who failed to believe in words given by Moses were wrapped around by the winding sheets of sand, what will not be the fate of those who refuse the

words of Christ! The author also pointed out the cure, so that they might not fall into this wickedness, and that was, to *exhort one another.* "Exhort one another daily" literally "beg""entreat""beseech" or "encourage one another."

"For we are made partakers of Christ," (3:14-16)
He commends them for having begun well; but lest, under the pretext of the grace which they had obtained, they should indulge themselves in carnal security, he says that there was need of perseverance; for many having only tasted the Gospel, do not think of any progress as though they had reached the summit. To partake of the great blessings Jesus provides, we must be steadfast, hold fast, and not give up until the end. "Today" we must hear his voice and not harden our hearts (compare verse 13). We must not be like those in the rebellion – i.e., the Israelites described in verses 7-11. Verse 15 quotes again verses 7, 8 and serves as a transition from verse 14 to verse 16.The phrase *"For some, when they had heard",* means that David spoke of the fathers as though that whole generation were unbelieving; but it appears that some who truly feared God mingled with the wicked. The apostle mentions this to alter what had been more severely said by David, in order that we may know that the word is preached to all the people so that all those who obey should live.We must exhort one another and not fall away. It is not

enough to start serving Jesus. We must keep on till the end.

"They did not enter into his rest because of unbelief" (3:17- 19)

The "rest" referred to here is clearly shown, by context, to be the promised land of Canaan.REST means Cessation from work that has been well done. Not a relief from fatigue. The hardening of heart was brought about by the deceitfulness of sin. Because of their sin, the Israelites could not enter God's rest. The sin mentioned is the sin of unbelief that is willful unbelief. Further note that verse 18 says the people could not enter because of *disobedience*, but verse 19 says it was because of *unbelief.* This shows that unbelief and disobedience go hand in hand. Their lack of trust in God led to a lack of doing what God said. Note that the people could not enter because of their own disobedience and unfaithfulness. It was not because the enemies were so strong or because God had failed to provide what they needed. They died in the wilderness.

Hebrews 4

G. Jesus is better than Joshua (Hebrews 4:1-13)

"Let us therefore fear," (vs.1)This is the first appearance of the exhortation "let us," which occurs 13 times in Hebrews (4:1, 11, 14, 16; 6:1; 10:22, 23, 24; 12:1[twice], 28; 13:13, 15).The word *fear* which is mentioned is not that which shakes the confidence of faith. It is the kind of fear that fills us with such concern that we grow not stagnant with indifference. Let us then fear, not that we ought to tremble or to entertain distrust as though uncertain as to the issue, but lest we be unfaithful to God's grace. The author used the term "rest" as Moses did, as an equivalent to ceasing from the work of fulfilling God's will and entering into all the inheritance that God promised His peopleBy saying Lest we be disappointed of the promise left us, he intimates that no one comes short of it except he who by rejecting grace has first renounced the promise; for God is so far from repenting to do us good that he ceases not to bestow his gifts except when we despise his calling.These verses evidently state the point the author is making as he continues to discuss God's refusal to allow the Israelites to enter Canaan because of their sins.

"For unto us was the gospel preached," (vs.2) But the Israelites did not profit from the message given them

because they did not respond in faith. They heard but did not believe strongly enough to obey (Read 3:18, 19). What is the "gospel "that both the Israelites and the original readers of this letter had heard preached to them? It was probably the gospel about their inheritance and the possibility of entering into their "rest."So, there was not a mixture of both hearing and faith. The gospel of Canaan's rest was preached to Israel but availed nothing, because the hearers were destitute of faith. They said, *"Can God?"* instead of saying, *"God can!"* They thought of their enemies as giants and themselves as grasshoppers, because they left God out of account. Take God into account -and we are giants and our enemies grasshoppers.The point then is that the Hebrews (and we) must believe God's word to the point of obeying it, else we too will not benefit from the gospel.

1. The better rest

Two fundamental truths are presented in this passage.
(a) God has a rest. (4:3-7)
It is God`s rest because it is of His providing. Israel had forfeited Canaan rest through unbelief.The rest Israel did *not* enter was the land of Canaan. They *did* receive the 7th-day Sabbath rest, as already noted (see 3:16-19). So, the rest that remains for us is not the 7th-day Sabbath. The 7th day then is simply introduced as an illustration of rest, showing that God rested after His work. He expected His people to be able to likewise rest in

Canaan. But they could not rest there because they failed to do the work He commanded. People have a right to rest only after they have completed their work, like God completed His. The people did not accomplish the work God required of them, so He did not allow them to enter into His rest in Canaan.

The expression in verse 3 is confusing: "although the works were finished from the foundation of the world." I am not quite sure of the point; but the following is at least valid, though I am not sure it is the point the author is making.

(b) This Rest is to be enjoyed by His People. (4:8-11)

Therefore verses 1, 6-9 show that there is a "rest" remaining for God's people (Redemption rest) which is spiritual and eternal. Redemption rest is external faith resting upon the infallible word of God. Faith believes what God has said. We will enter that rest like God entered His rest after He completed the work of creation (Creation rest) verse 4 and this Rest was marred by sin.This definitely does not teach that the 7th-day Sabbath is binding on Christian's today, as but was binding on Israel. If that is the rest referred to here, they did enter it. But the Sabbath that remains for us is compared to the one they did not enter into. (Redemption rest) When, therefore, they obtained possession of it, they ought not to have rested as though they had attained to the summit of their wishes, but on the contrary to meditate on what as spiritual as by it suggested. They to whom David addressed the Psalm were in possession of that land, but they were reminded of the duty of seeking a better rest. (Redemption rest) We then see how the land of Canaan was a rest (Canaan rest) verse 8 which was interrupted by hostile powers; it was indeed but evanescent, beyond which it was the duty of the faithful to advance. In this sense the Apostle denies that that rest was given by Joshua; for the people under his guidance entered the Promised Land (Canaan rest) for this end, that they might with greater eagerness advance forward towards (Redemption rest) heaven. Yet this event cannot be the fulfilment of "rest" that David referred to because, many years after Joshua, David still spoke of a rest remaining for the people (Redemption rest). It follows that the rest that Israel entered in Canaan was just one of the Old Testament types or symbols of the greater rest that remains for those who are faithful under the New Testament (Redemption rest). David's statement makes this clear. In receiving this rest, God's people will cease from work in a manner similar to God's resting on the Sabbath (verse 10).

The author exhorts them in two-fold ways:

(a) Let us not fear, lest we should miss it.

(b)Let us labour so that we many win it. (vs. 11)

The author brings out three things to our attention: (Verses 6-8)

(a) Israel under Moses forfeited the rest of Canaan.

(b) Israel under Joshua entered Canaan, but was

temporal, physical and material.

(c) the Canaan rest under Joshua was not final since God spoke of a rest in David's time which was long after the rest of Canaan.

The Hebrews must take care not to be led away from the gospel back to the Old Testament. God was displeased with people who sinned under that law. If they returned to it, there was no guarantee of pleasing God. Perhaps they thought God would always be pleased with them if they were under that law. The writer shows that even that law stated that God was not always pleased with those who were under it. He also shows God will punish them if they now reject His new law.

Chapters 3 & 4 refer several times to "rest" for God's people, but the word used is not the word for the Sabbath. Verse 9 uses a word with a similar root as "sabbath," but it is a different word. The common word for the Sabbath day [sabbaton] is not used anywhere in Hebrews 4. The word for "rest" in verse 9 [sabbatismos] is used only here, and the context shows that it describes rest, not a particular day of rest.

Standard translations of 4:9 say God's people will receive a "rest" (KJV, NKJV) or "Sabbath rest" (ASV) or "Sabbath rest" (NASB, NIV, ESV). No standard translation of verse 9 says "Sabbath *day*." They all emphasize the idea of *rest*, not the idea of a "day."

Thayer says the word in Hebrews 4:9 means: "the blessed rest from toils and troubles looked for in the age to come by the true worshipers of God and true Christians." Thayer is a fallible human, but the point is that verse 9 does not use the word for the 7th-day Sabbath. To demonstrate, consider the difference in English between "Sabbath day" and "sabbatical." These words have the same root, but they differ because they refer to different ideas. Both imply a rest or break, but a "sabbatical" may be of any duration or frequency. Only context can determine. Likewise, the word in Hebrews 4:9 could refer to any period of rest, regardless of when it happens, how often it happens, or how long it lasts.

2. The three phases of Rest

(a) Verses 4, 10 refer to God resting on the 7th day when creation was complete. But verses 9, 10 shows that the parallel between this and the "rest" promised to God's people refers simply the idea of *resting* or ceasing work. Nothing says God's *people* here rest on any particular *day*.

(b) In context, chapters 3 & 4 discuss Israel's failure to enter the rest God had promised them in Canaan. Note the repeated references to not "entering" the "rest" – 3:11, 18, 19; 4:3, 5. This point was first stated in Psalms 95:7-11, which is quoted in Hebrews 3:7-11 and explained in 3:16-19. God had promised that Israel would receive "rest" when they "entered" the promised land of Canaan – Exodus 33:14; Deut. 3:20; 12:9,10; 25:19; Joshua 1:11-15; 21:44. But those who left Egypt

under Moses' leadership were disobedient, so God
decreed that they would not enter that rest but would
wander in the wilderness forty years. See Numbers
14:23, 28-30; Deut. 1:34, 35. Note that none of this had
anything to do with the 7th-day Sabbath. Israel did
receive the command to keep the Sabbath day. But
Hebrews 3, 4 discusses a rest that God promised to them
but they did *not* enter because of their rebellion against
Him in the wilderness.

3) Likewise, the context admonishes God's people today
to learn from Israel's failure. Note 4:1 – As with Israel,
*the context discusses a "promise" God's people seek to
"enter," not a command to be observed, remembered, or
kept holy.* Note again the repeated references to our
"entering" the "rest" God has prepared – 4:1,
3,6,9,10,11.

3:12-15; 4:1-11 explain that, even after Israel finally
entered Canaan under Joshua's leadership, still David
had later predicted (in Psalms 95) a "rest" that awaits
God's people. We must not imitate Israel's disobedience
or we too will not "enter" the "rest" that God has for us,
but we can enter that rest if we hold fast to the end.

3. The Sabbath day as a shadow

We will see, as the book of Hebrews proceeds, that Old
Testament institutions and practices were symbols of the
new covenant (Hebrews 8:5; 9:23; 10:1). The Old
Testament service was not given by God as the final goal

or permanent plan He had for man. The first covenant was merely a copy or shadow of the heavenly things, so they ceased when the new covenant came into effect. The Sabbath day had special significance to the nation of Israel (Exodus 31:13). The Sabbath day symbolized two things to Israel: the completion of the creation and God's rest on the seventh day and also God's deliverance of Israel from Egyptian captivity (Exodus 20:11; Deuteronomy 5:15). So the Sabbath had a double meaning: rest and deliverance.

This then symbolized Israel's entrance into rest when they entered into the land of Canaan after they were delivered from Egypt (Deuteronomy 12:9,10). This in turn became a symbol of our rest in heaven because we have been delivered from the bondage of sin (Hebrews 4:1-11).

This deliverance and rest was accomplished by the sacrifice of Jesus on the cross. The Sabbath was symbolic of our deliverance from sin and our eternal rest accomplished by the death of Jesus on the cross. So the Sabbath, along with other Old Testament symbols, had accomplished their purpose and ceased to be binding when Jesus died on the cross.

4. The Redemption Rest For God's People

Matthew 11:28,29 – Jesus promised to give "rest" to the souls of those who labor and are heavy laden, if they will take His yoke upon them. The book of Revelation 14:13 shows that those who die in the Lord "rest from their labors," just like Hebrews 4:10. The unfaithful, however, have no "rest" (verse 11). 2 Thessalonians 1:7 – The faithful will be given "rest" when Jesus is revealed from heaven, but those who do not obey the gospel will receive tribulation, etc. (verses 6,8,9). Just like Hebrews 4, all these verses promise "rest" to God's faithful people – a rest that the disobedient do not receive. No one would think that any of these verses have anything to do with a command to observe a specific day of the week. And neither does Hebrews 4. We seek to receive rest to our souls: eternal rest in heaven. This is a *promise*– a blessing we may *enter* after we have been faithful – not a *command* we must obey. The reference to God's rest does not bind a day on us; it simply means He rested from His work, and someday we too will rest from ours. If we can see that the "rest" Israel failed to enter is not the same as God's 7th day rest, and if we can see that the rest Israel failed to enter is not the same rest awaiting us, we should be able to see that the rest awaiting us is likewise similar to, but not the same as, God's 7th day rest.

To use this context to argue that people today must keep the 7th-day Sabbath is a patent error. One of the main points of the book of Hebrews is that the First Covenant has been done away and replaced by the gospel. To go back to binding that Old Testament would constitute exactly the error the author is teaching us to avoid! To use the book to try to bind the Old Law not only misses the point of the context, it flatly contradicts it! See again Hebrews 10:1-10; 7:11-14; 8:6-13; 9:1-4; Colossians 2:13-17; 2 Corinthians 3:6-11; Galatians 3:24,25; 5:1-6; Romans 7:1-7; Ephesians 2:11-16.

5. God's word is powerful (4:12, 13)

There is no escape for disobedience and unbelief, because we have to do with the omniscience of God. The conception of 4:12-13 is of a victim appointed for sacrifice and thrown upon its back, that the keen edge of the knife may do its work more readily. The divine scrutiny is still sharper. There is so much of the soul in what we do, that is, of our opinions and activities. The author has shown that the people must not go back to the Old Testament. To do so would be to fall away from God and miss His reward, even as Israel did. One must not think He can fall away and yet escape such condemnation, for God's word is powerful and must be respected and obeyed (Romans. 1:16; Isaiah 55:10, 11). It is powerful enough to show men their errors now, convicting us of sin and piercing our consciences with guilt. Then at the judgment, it will be the standard of judgment and will show us to be worthy of death if we do not obey (John 12:48; Romans 2:16).

So, the word is said to be living and powerful, sharper than a two-edged sword (compare Ephesians 6:17; Revelation 1:16; 2:12; 19:15, 23). The word can divide soul and spirit, joints and marrow (1 Thessalonians

5:23). Even as a sword can pierce to the innermost parts of the body, so the word can pierce to the innermost parts of the soul (Acts 2:37). You can hide nothing from God. God distinguishes between these and those promptings of His Spirit which are really important and influential. Only what is born of the Spirit will stand the test of eternity!

Shall we not fail in that scrutiny? Will he not detect in us that evil heart of unbelief? We need not fear; because our High Priest has passed the veil that hides the invisible and eternal and has entered the divine presence. "Mercy and grace to help in time of need!" will meet our supreme needs-mercy for our sins, grace for our helplessness and frailty.

II. The High Priesthood of Jesus (4:14-8:6)

A. Jesus is better than Aaron

"Let us hold fast our profession," (vs.14) The author now proceeds by emphasizing the greatness of Jesus and His high priesthood. As it was discussed earlier of Jesus, this should show us more reasons why we should remain with the gospel and not leave it. He opens his discourse with another definite declaration that we should hold fast

our confession of Jesus. We have been given several reasons to hold fast our confession, and will be given many more (2:1ff; 3:6-4:13). One of the reasons we should continue to hold fast is that Jesus is our High Priest. However, we have obtained more privileges with Him as High Priest than our fathers under the Old Covenant.

There are three things noted in verse 15:

Priests served as representatives acting on behalf of the people in worship to God. They could not properly appeal to God on the people's behalf if they did not understand or sympathize with the people's conditions. Our High Priest was *"touched with the feeling of our infirmities"* (vs.15). In Greek this sentence is one word, [sumpathesai] from which we get sympathy. Only used twice with another reference in Hebrews 10:34 translated "Compassion." "To sympathize" is to feel with." He sympathizes with our infirmities not with our sins. Infirmities are the sinless consequences of sin such as sorrows of life, physical limitations, bereavement, sickness and grief etc.

"But was in all points tempted like as we are," (vs.15) Our Lord Jesus was tempted in all points like we are. He was actually a man in the sense of experiencing temptation and all the kinds of troubles we do. Throughout His lifetime, some people persistently tried to catch Him in His words. They often mocked and belittled Him. He left all the glories of heaven just to

identify himself with sinners, He had no home and He died as a criminal rejected by all society and betrayed by his friends. There is no type of hardship any of us can experience that was not experienced at least in some related form by Jesus. Nevertheless, the major point of the author here is that Jesus' suffering was needed for us to know that He understands and is concerned of all our affliction and troubles. Therefore, we will be bold and confident to go to Him to meet our need for grace and mercy (verse 15). Everyone as tempted (enticed) when he is drawn away of his own lust and enticed. Our Lord was tempted. He was tested or tried. (Hungered, thirsted, had pain, weariness and loneliness)

"Yet without sin," (vs.15) "Yet" here is misleading in the Authorized Version. The literal translation reads "without sin" or "apart from sin." (4:14 and 9:28) Temptation does not involve sin.Jesus was tempted as we are, but He did not sin. "Apart from" signifies having no connection or relationship to. The phrase "Without sin" appears twice in Hebrews (4:15; 9:28) "without" or "apart from" denotes an entire absence of sin. Jesus had to be sinless in order to offer the kind of sacrifice we needed. (1 Peter 2:21-22)

"Let us therefore come boldly," (vs.16) The author asserts that access to God is open to all who come to him relying on Christ the Mediator; he now encourages the faithful to endeavor without any hesitation to present themselves before God. They certainly say that God is to

be required; except that the way by which it is possible to come to him is not pointed out, and the gate is barred by which alone men can enter. "We have a high priest who is willing to help us; therefore we may come bold and without any hesitation to the throne of grace."

Hebrews 5

B. Qualifications for a Priest (5:1-4)

Hebrew 5: 1-4 states the four qualifications for a Jewish
high priest as follows:

1. He was to be a man

"For every high priest taken from among men," (vs.1)
The author is comparing Christ with the Levitical priests
as he teaching us the similarities and the differences.
Therefore, the priest was a representative of the people
in spiritual matters of worship to God. When the author
writes, "every high priest," he points out that the role;
the duty and appointment of the high priest are all
governed by divine standards. That means the office of
high priest works according to the scripture. He is to
showing what Christ's office really is, and also he is
proving that whatever was ordained under the law was
ordained on his account. Human priests had this
qualification because they were themselves subject to
temptation. In fact, like other people they gave in to
temptation and sinned. The High Priest has solidarity
with people as he is taken from among then. The Old
Testament principle has to do with both the identity of
the High Priest with the people and the distinction made

between the Priests and the people. At that time a High Priest had to be a man. God did not choose angels to be priests because they don't have the nature of men. Only a man can rightly minister on behalf of men. On the Day of Atonement the High Priest must offer a special sacrifice for himself and for his household before he offers sacrifice for the people because the priests from men are subject to weakness. His weakness enables him to deal gently with those who are ignorant and going astray. (V.2)

2. He was called of God

"....but he that is called of God," (vs.4) A true Priest had to be appointed by God. He had to be a God's man-not simply in the sense of being faithful and obedient to God but in the sense of being selected by God. God appointed him on behalf of men. Only those that were called of God served in this office. These high priest appointees were primarily "Aaron" and his successors. This ceased to be true after Israel lost her sovereignty as a nation, beginning with the Babylonian Captivity. After that the high priesthood became a political appointment.

(Numbers 16; 1 Samuel 13:8-14; 2 Chronicles 26:16-21).No one takes the honor to himself but receives it when God calls him just as Aaron was.

3. He was to be sympathetic

"Who can have compassion," (vs.2) Therefore, they needed to offer sacrifice for themselves as well as for the people of Israel. The priests therefore, could have compassion for sinners. One characteristic a priest needed was the ability to sympathize with the people. (4:15) If he was to represent the people before God, he needed to be able to see the people's viewpoint. Particularly, a priest needed compassion for the sins and weaknesses of the people he was representing. The people could not go directly and personally to God with their offerings. They had to take them to the priest who would offer them to God. He was the Mediator between God and the people.

4. **Was to offer Sacrifice for men as a representative of People**

The High Priest represents people in matters related to God especially offering gifts and sacrifices. A High Priest shares in the general duties performed by all the Priests. The High Priest offers sacrifices on the Day of Atonement when he takes two goats and a ram from among the Israelites. He acts before God as a representative of people making expiation of their sins.

C. Jesus the Perfect High Priest (5:5-10)

Hebrews 5: 5-10 shows how Jesus met all the qualifications of High Priest.

1. Jesus had to be a man

"Thou art my Son," (vs.5) For though Jesus was
begotten of God the Father, he was not on this account
made also a priest. The same God who appointed Jesus
as His "Son" also appointed Him as "high priest" forever.
(cf. 6:20; 7:17, 21, 24, 28) Now, what sort of Son did
God manifest to us? One indued with no honor, with no
power? Nay, one who was to be a Mediator between
himself and man; his begetting then included his
priesthood. [4] We have a Great High Priest, Jesus the Son
of God and it is while He is Son that He carries out His
work of high priest. The begetting of Jesus, of whom the

---

4 This passage, "Thou art my Son," etc., in this place, is only
adduced to show that Christ was the Son of

God: Christ did not honor or magnify or exalt himself, (for so
δοξάζω means here,) but he who said to him, "Thou art my son,"
etc., did honor or exalt him. This is the meaning of the sentence. The
verse may thus be rendered, — **5.** So also Christ, himself he did not
exalt to be a high priest, but he who had said to him, "My son art
thou, I have this day begotten thee." It is the same as though he had
said, "Christ did not make himself a high priest but God." And the
reason why he speaks of God as having said "My Son," etc., seems
to be this, — to show that he who made him king (for the reference
in Psalm 2 is to his appointment as a king) made him also a high
priest. And this is confirmed by the next quotation from Psalm 110;
for in the first verse he is spoken of as a king, and then in verse 4 his
priesthood is mentioned.

Psalmist speaks, was a testimony which the Father rendered to him before men. (Psalm 2; Psalm 110)

"Thou *art* a priest forever," (vs.7)" When ... Jerusalem fell into David's hands and became his capital city (II Sam. 5:6ff.), he and his heirs became successors to Melchizedek's kingship, and probably also (in a titular capacity at least) to the priesthood of God Most High."[5]

"Who in the days of his flesh," (vs.7) A true High Priest had to be a man. This was acceptable and clear to Jews. But they had the problem with the incarnation of God becoming man. Jesus, who is God, could not be a true High Priest unless He was a man. Jesus entered into the human world and felt everything that men will ever feel. Hence, that the Son of God has a nature in common with us, does not diminish his dignity, but commends it the more to us; for he is fitted to reconcile us to God, because he is man. Let this mind be in you, which was also in Christ Jesus: Who, being in the form of God, thought it not robbery to be equal with God: But made himself of no reputation, and took upon him the form of a servant, and was made in the likeness of men: And being found in fashion as a man, he humbled himself, and became obedient unto death, even the death of the cross. (Philippians 2:6) Therefore Paul, in order to prove that he is a Mediator, expressly calls him man; for had he been taken from among angels or any other beings, we

---

[5]3Moffatt, p. 64.

could not by him be united to God, as he could not react down to us. Jesus became human so He could sympathize with our needs. He offered the only perfect sacrifice for sins which was not offered for Himself but only for us.

"When he had offered up prayers," (Vs 7) If Christ had not been touched by sorrow; no comfort could arise to us from his sufferings. However, when we hear that he also endured the pain of mind, the likeness becomes then evident to us. Christ did not go through death and other evils because he disregarded them or was pressed down by no feeling of distress, but he prayed with tears through which he testified the severe anguish of his soul. "Father, if it be possible, let this cup pass from me," (Matthew 26:42; Luke 22:42) and also to another, "My God, my God, why hast thou forsaken me?" (Matthew 27:46) It is indeed certain that he was reduced to great straits; and being overwhelmed with real sorrows, he earnestly prayed his Father to bring him help. [6]

2. Jesus was Sympathetic with men

Hebrews 5: 7-8 says Jesus was sympathetic with men. He was himself a man as any High Priest served in the

---

6 Stuart on this passage very justly observes, "If Jesus died as a common virtuous suffered, and merely as a martyr to the truth, without any vicarious suffering laid upon him, then is his death a most unaccountable event in respect to the manner of his behavior while suffering it; and it must be admitted that multitudes of humble.

temple. He offered up both prayer and supplications because of the anguish he faced in becoming Sin for those who believed in Him. If he had not experienced human feelings and pains, he could not have been a sympathetic High Priest.

3. Jesus offered Sacrifice for men

"......when he had offered," (vs.7) There are two things that are mentioned which gifts and sacrifices; the first word includes, diverse kinds of sacrifices, and is therefore a general term; but the second denotes especially the sacrifices of expiation. This meant that the priest without a sacrifice is no peacemaker between God and man, for without a sacrifice sins are not atoned for, nor is the wrath of God pacified. In his suffering and death Jesus fulfilled the last requirement for High Priest.Jesus suffered on earth. He offered prayers and supplications with fervent cries and tears especially in Gethsemane and on the cross (Matthew 26:39-44; 27:46, 50; Luke 22:41, 44; Psalm 22:1). In the garden of Gethsemane, an angel came to strengthen Him (Luke 22:43) and on the cross, he prayed for those who crucified Him to have the opportunity to be forgiven for they did not know what they were doing.

Jesus' suffering was especially difficult because He knew that it could have been stopped. He offered himself as sacrifice and thus he became a perfect High Priest and source of eternal salvation. In offering sacrifices, Jesus differed in two ways from other priests.

Firstly, he did not have to make a sacrifice for himself and secondly, his sacrifice was once and for all. You may assume that the Son of God would never have to endure such suffering; but though He was God's Son, yet he did have to suffer obediently. (Philippians 2:5-8; Hebrews 2:10) He learned it in the sense of personally experiencing all that it required.

"Yet learned he obedience," (vs.8) The author says Christ's suffering was as a result to accustom himself to obedience; not that he was driven to this by force. He was willing to provide to his Father the obedience which he owed. Therefore, Christ by his death learned fully what it was to obey God, since he was then led in an unusual way of denying himself through renouncing his own will, to the will of his Father. As shown in Luke 22:42 that Jesus said, "Father, if thou be willing, remove this cup from me: nevertheless not my will, but thine, be done."

"And being made perfect," (Vs.9) The verb *Sanctified,* suits this passage better than "made perfect." The Greek word [τελειωθεὶς] means both; but as he speaks here of the priesthood, he rightfully mentions sanctification. The Lord Jesus Christ himself in John 17:19 said, "For their sakes I sanctify myself." It hence appears that this is to be properly applied to his human nature, in which he performed the office of a priest, and in which he also suffered. [7]

"....unto all them that obey him," (Vs.9) If then we are yearning that Christ's obedience should be of great benefit to us, we must emulate him; for here the author means that its benefit shall come to those who obey.

4. Jesus was appointed by God

"Called of God an high priest," (vs.10) Jesus was chosen, sent and honored by the Father God. Again the author quotes from the Old Testament, " Thou art my Son, today I have begotten thee and thou art a priest for ever according to the order of Melchizedek", to support his point. Jesus' claim to priesthood is confirmed by Psalms 110:4. Jesus had been called God's Son in Psalms 2:7, which had been formerly quoted in Hebrews 1:5 (compare Acts 13:33). In a similar way He was called by God to be a priest in Psalms 110. The Jewish Hebrew readers knew that these two passages referred to Messiah. They knew that the Messiah was to be a great king and Priest appointed by God.

---

7 The word τελειωθεὶς, means here the same as in chapter 2:10. Stuart gives it the same meaning here as in the former passage, "Then when exalted to glory," etc.; but this does not comport with what follows, for it was not his exaltation to glory that qualified him to be "the author (or the causer or effecter) of eternal salvation," but his perfect or complete work in suffering, by his having completely and perfectly performed the work of atonement. And that his suffering in obedience to God's will, even his vicarious suffering, is meant here, appears also from the following reference to his being a priest after the order of Melchisedec. The meaning then seems to be, that Christ having fully completed his work as a priest, and that by suffering, became thereby the author of eternal salvation.

D. The Sin of Apostasy (5:11-6:20)

1. Failing to mature (5:11-14)

"....he first principles of the oracles of God;" (vs.12)
Christians are expected, not just to apply the word to
their own lives, but also to teach it to others in different
capacities. (2 Timothy 2:2, 24-26; Acts 8:4; Ephesians
4:15, 16; Hebrews 10:24f; 3:12-14; etc) If years go by
and we still are unable to teach, something is wrong and
we are worthy of rebuke. "Oracle" means "a Divine
response or utterance, an oracle" – Vine. Verse 12
introduced the concept of milk versus meat in God's
word. This is here explained to mean that those who are
immature in understanding will only be able to
understand the basics of the gospel, just as a physical
baby can only digest milk. We have seen that they were
facing temptation to fall away from the gospel and go
back to the Old Covenant. The author has repeatedly
admonished them to hold fast to the truth and not drift
away or go into apostasy. They had learned basic truth,
but their knowledge of truth had not grown. As a result,
they were in danger of complete apostasy.

"For every one that useth milk is unskillful," (vs.13)
Some things are harder to understand and some are
easier. One who is mature is able to understand more
difficult things, just like a full-grown person can digest

meat. *"But strong meat belongeth to them,"* *(vs.14)* (Compare Matthew 28:19, 20; 1 Corinthians 3:1-3; Ephesians 4:14-16; 1 Peter 2:2; 2 Peter 3:15, 16) There is no problem with being a baby spiritually, if a person was just born again recently. In fact, this is the normal, expected circumstance. We do not expect a physical baby to be able to digest meat, and we should not expect a new Christian to be able to understand deeper issues in the gospel. But when one has been a Christian for years and still is so immature in knowledge that he is unable to handle deeper subjects, then it is clear he has not been studying as he should, and he should be ashamed of himself. He is like a physically grown adult who has not matured to eat meat so must continually be fed milk from a bottle! We are also taught here that, in order to discern or recognize or discriminate between good and evil, one must have exercised his senses by reason of use. In other words, understanding right from wrong takes time and growth. It also takes study. And it takes an open mind. And it takes *practice* and *experience.* (1 Timothy 4:7f) Often those who are older and more experienced in *applying* God's word will be able to see a sin or danger far more quickly than those who are younger. In fact, two people may be equally familiar with a passage of Scripture, yet one may see a valid application of that Scripture to a situation, where the other does not see it. The difference may simply be a matter of experience.

Hebrews 6

2. Principles of the Doctrine of Christ (6:1-3)

"let us go on unto perfection,"(vs.1) The Hebrew Christians were not mature in their knowledge as they ought to have been, so it was hard for the author to get them to understand what he needed to say. He has rebuked them for this. The author compares such attitudes to people who lay the foundation of a building, and then instead of building on that foundation, they just keep working over and over on the foundation. But all they ever have is a foundation: no building. What good is it? We should "go on to perfection." (maturity) But remember that 5:12-14 associated maturity with being able to eat meat. Those who are able to handle only first principles clearly are not mature. Therefore, they need to go on to perfection. So the author said the people should go on beyond these basic teachings, and he said he intended to do this. The word "perfection" (vs.1) is translated "Maturity" here. To remain or to return to the Old Covenant with its symbols and sacrifices, demonstrated that these Hebrews were immature. He is encouraging them to leave the shadows and go for perfection. For these Hebrew Christians, going back to the Old Covenant would be laying again the foundation; that is, the principles of the doctrine of Christ (Levitical rituals). The word "perfection" appears 13 times in the epistle, translated 12 times from Greek word [teleos] this

letter "to equip or mature." (2:10; 5:9; 7:11; 19, 28; 9:9;
10;1,14; 11:40; 12:2,23) It is found once, translated from
the word, [katartitzo] meaning: to adjust." (13:21)
The author describes this foundation as follows:

(a) Of repentance from dead works and of faith towards God (vs.1)

God was constantly calling the Hebrews back to
repentance because their works were dead works. The
Gentiles were commanded to repent from sin (Acts 8:22)
yet Hebrews were commanded to repent from dead
works. The author referred Dead works to the works of
the law which are of no benefit as regards to obtaining
eternal life. (Galatians 3:11-12, Colossians 2:16-18) The
Hebrew Christians should no longer rest in dead works
of the law but should grow in faith towards God through
Christ and His finished work on the cross which brings
eternal life.

(b) Of the doctrine of baptisms (vs.2)

The author is describing Judaism in its ritual character.
He then explains the term "Baptisms" in this context as
the same Greek word translated "washings (9:1-10)
which refers to ceremonial washings or ablutions of
Judaism. These baptisms had to do with the sprinkling of
the blood by priests and during propitiation on the
atonement day by the high priest, the washing of the
Laver and other ceremonial ordinances connected with
outward approach to God. "And he shall kill the bullock

before the LORD: and the priests, Aaron's sons, shall bring the blood, and sprinkle the blood round about upon the altar that is by the door of the tabernacle of the congregation." (Lev 1:5) "But his inwards and his legs shall he wash in water: and the priest shall burn all on the altar, to be a burnt sacrifice, an offering made by fire, of a sweet savour unto the LORD. (Lev 1:9) (Read Leviticus 16:1-34) This was a typical cleansing of the conscience from dead works in order to serve the living and true God (9:14) by the washing of the regeneration and renewing of the Holy Spirit. (Titus 3:5)

3… and of Laying on of hands (vs.2)

The laying of hands, closely connected with baptisms, is not Christian laying on of hands. This refers to the imposition of the hands by the offerer upon the sacrificial offering."And he shall put his hand upon the head of the burnt offering; and it shall be accepted for him to make atonement for him" (Lev 1:4).The fate of the scapegoat was very moving! Laden with the sins of the people, it is led forth through the crowd of penitents; innocent yet execrated, dumb yet eloquent of the doom of the sin bearer, escaping death by the knife, to be forsaken even unto death! So Jesus died, with the cry of "Forsaken" on His lips. "And Aaron shall lay both his hands upon the head of the live goat, and confess over him all the iniquities of the children of Israel, and all their transgressions in all their sins, putting them upon the head of the goat, and shall send him away by the hand of a fit man into the wilderness: And the goat shall bear upon him all their iniquities unto a land not inhabited: and he shall let go the goat in the wilderness."(Lev 16:21-22)

4. And of the resurrection of the dead and of eternal judgment (vs.2)

It was an Old Testament doctrine as well. (Daniel 12:2; Job 19:25) The Jews in the days of the author, were divided in their opinion with regards to the resurrection of the saints (Philippians 3:11).The Old Covenant was one of perpetual sacrifices, a remembering of sins every year but no remission of sins, thus offering only eternal judgments, contrast to the New Covenant (Hebrews 10:14).Jesus, the resurrection and the life, speaks in Isaiah 26:19. What comfort results to those that dwell in the dust of self-abasement and despair to look up to the ever-living Christ, from whom streams of life-giving energy come to believing hearts! Arise and sing, thou broken heart: even now the stone is being rolled from the door of thy sepulcher; the morning dew is distilling upon thee. The hope of resurrection, of the life beyond the darkness of their times, animated the hearts of the Chosen People. In the same way the Apostle Paul refers to it in 1Cor15:58.The Resurrection was primarily not a doctrine but a *fact*. It is not necessary to argue it, but simply to *say* that Christ arose, therefore all will arise, because Christ is the Son of man. Other religions rest on foundations of philosophy and metaphysics, but the empty grave in Joseph's garden is the keystone.

3. Apostasy: Rejecting Christ (6:4-6)

"For it is impossible for those," (vs.4) Apostasy is an intentional falling away or withdrawal and is the most serious of all sins because it is the most deliberate and willful form of unbelief. Apostle Paul speaks of a large falling away when he cautions Thessalonians not to be misled about the coming of the Lord, for it will not come unless the apostasy comes first. 2 Thessalonians 2:3. Jesus clearly spoke of the same apostasy in Matthew 24: 10. Apostasy is determined by what you leave, not where you go after you leave. Apostasy can also be defined as receiving knowledge of the truth but willfully remaining in sin. An apostate has seen and heard the truth but will fully rejects it. It is not a sin of ignorance, but of rejecting the known truth. Holding on to the old covenant brings a person to apostasy. Many of the unbelieving Jews addressed in the book of Hebrews were very much in this danger. Their religion not only would not bring them salvation, but had become an obstacle to salvation. Religious tradition is a great hindrance, which cause apostasy. The statement, *"it is impossible if they shall fall away to renew them again unto repentance"* does not refer to Christians who; have developed cold in their Christian experience, who have been unfaithful in service and have failed in time of temptation. This is

because these Christians have hope but the statement refers to the Hebrew Christians who are departing from the New Covenant truths and returning back to Judaism.

The phrase *"once enlightened."*(Vs.4) literally, *"once for all enlightened"*. *"Once"* meaning *"once for all"* is found in 9:7, 26-28; 10:2; 12:26-27.Similarly, the word *once* that is used to speak of those who "have once been enlightened" is the Greek term [ἅπαξ] which is used, for example, in Philippians 4:16 of the Philippians' sending Paul a gift *"once* and again," and in Hebrews 9:7 of entrance in the Holy of Holies *"once* a year." Therefore, this word does not mean that something happened "once" and can never be repeated, but simply that it happened once, without specifying whether it will be repeated or not. They were enlightened through the revelation of God in Christ, the true light and through the power of the Holy Spirit. In the Old Testament "enlightened" is usually translated "taught" or "instructed. (Psalm 119:130; 2 Kings 12:2; 17:27) Compare New Testament (John 1:9; Ephesians 1:18; 3:9 and Hebrews 10:32). The word *enlightened* translates the Greek term [φωτίζω] which refers to learning in general, not necessarily a learning that results in salvation it is used in John 1:9 of "enlightening" every man that comes into the world, in 1 Cor. 4:5 of the enlightening that comes at the final judgment, and in Eph. 1:18 of the enlightening that accompanies growth in the Christian life. The word is not a "technical term" that means that the people in question were saved.

The text further says that these people *"have tasted the heavenly gift"* and that they "have *tasted* the goodness of the word of God and the powers of the age to come" (vv4–5). Inherent in the idea of tasting is the fact that the tasting is temporary and one might or might not decide to accept the thing that is tasted. For example, the same Greek word [γεύομαι] is used in Matthew 27:34 to say that those crucifying Jesus "offered him wine to drink, mingled with gall; but when he *tasted* it, he would not drink it." "They have consciously partaken of (Hebrews 2:9 and 1 Peter 2:3) "the Heavenly gift is the "Holy Spirit." the same Greek word translated "tasted" refers to complete appropriation. (e.g. Jesus Christ "tasted death" for everyone, 2:9; cf. 1 Pet. 2:1-3) This is an Old Testament usage as (cf. Ps. 34:8). Christians become "partakers" (cf. 1:9, "companions;" and 3:1, 14, "partakers" of the Holy Spirit through Spirit-baptism. "Heavenly gift" emphasizes the heavenly quality of this gift. The word tasted is also used as a figurative speech; meaning enlightened which translates the Greek term [φωτίζω].Tasted the word of God which is the gospel of Christ as preached (2:3, 4; Acts 5:20; John 6:63; Acts 11:14; 5:17, 26, 32; John 3:34; 6:63; Acts 11:14; 10:44).They tasted the power of age to come. The word "world" is literally translated "age" in which we're living (millennial age).

"If they shall fall away," (vs.6) The Phrase to fall away literally means "to deviate," "to turn aside" (Ezekiel 14:13; 15:8). By failing from the New Covenant back to Old Covenant, the Hebrews are crucifying to themselves the Son of God afresh and put him in an open shame. The phrase *"put to an open shame"* literally means "to make example of" or "To make a public show." (Numbers 25:4)

"For the earth which drinketh in the rain," (vs.7) Here is an illustration showing what will happen to those who are disobedient as described in verses 4-6. People are like soil that can produce what is good and useful or can produce what is harmful and worthless. Similarly, people can produce fruits in their lives that are useful to the One who cultivates their ability to be fruitful (John 15:2). God will bless and reward them (this would indicate that He is the farmer seeking a crop from the soil). But other soil, receiving the same rain, can instead produce thorns and briars – worthless weeds. In this case, the ground is worthless, and the only thing to do is to burn it to destroy the worthless crops. (John 15:6; Matthew 13) So, the author warns these Hebrews that this is what God will do to them if they fall away and refuse to repent. God offers rich blessings to His people, making it possible for those who truly love Him to produce good crops of fruitful service.

"But, beloved, we are persuaded better things,"(vs.9) The word *"beloved"* is only found once in the book of

Hebrews and could be translated "divinely loved ones."
(1 Corinthians 10:14; 15:58; 2 Corinthians 7:1).The
word "persuaded" means" firmly convinced." (Vs. 4), "it
is impossible for those."Vs 6, "and if they shall fall
away." (Verse 9) The second person is used- "we are
persuaded better things of you". The emphasis is on
"you". Three things desired to be seen in their lives
diligence (faith and patience) (Mathew 13:17, Luke
22:15; Romans 8:24). The phrase "full assurance"
(vs.11) may be translated "full development." The word
hope (vs.11) is here to be taken for faith, because of its
affinity to it. The author, however, seems to have
designedly used it, because he was speaking of
perseverance. He wanted them to remain faithful to God,
while waiting patiently for Him to fulfil His promises to
them regarding their future inheritance (be "imitators of
those who through faith and patience inherit the
promises. Let us then know that true faith is ever
connected with hope and hope develops into assurance.
The word "patience" (vs.12) could be rendered
"longsuffering" 2 Timothy 3:10, and James 5:7. The
words literally "lengthy spirit"- not easily out of temper.
Many people are clear and strong in regard to their faith
but they fail in respect of patience.

4. The Basis for our Steadfastness (6:13-20)

"For when God made promise," (vs.13) The author after exhorting his hearers to be followers (imitators) of them who through faith and patience inherit the promise. Verse 12 gives an illustration of the long suffering of faith in the life of Abram. He returns to the subject by reminding these Hebrews of one of their heroes, one of the most familiar Old Covenant characters named Abraham. But Abraham's example is referred to, not because he is the only one, but because he is more illustrious than that of any other. For though Abraham had this faith in common with all the godly; yet it is not without reason that he is called the father of the faithful. Without doubt, he is one of those whose faith we should imitate. He specifically reminds them of one of the best-known Old Testament fact which is the promise of God to Abraham. God had made promises to Abraham regarding his descendants. They would multiply and be blessed, receive the land of Canaan, and through them all nations of the earth would be blessed. (Genesis 22:16-18; 12:3, 4; 18:18; 26:4) This blessing was so important, God not only promised it but He also made an oath of confirmation. (Read verse 16) This promise is culminated in Christ as shown by Acts 3:25, 26; Galatians 3:8, 9, 16, 29. He is the one through whom the ultimate blessing came: the blessing of forgiveness of sins. This great promise to Abraham is enjoyed by the Hebrews and by us in the gospel and only in the gospel. If they turned from the gospel back to the Old

Testament, they would lose this great benefit that their whole nation had been awaiting! The example of Abraham shows first that the promise of God is sure (11:9, 10). Acts 7:2; Genesis 12:1-3; 11:31, 32; Genesis 15:6; 16:16; 17:15-18; 21:1-5; 22:1-14; 22:16, 17.Thepatience of Abraham commenced from the date of the original promise.

"...blessing I will bless" (vs.14) This phrase is a Hebraism, emphasizing the idea continued in the verb.Men confirm their word, in the highest degree, by taking an oath. This was accepted under the law as a means to end dispute. (Exodus 22:11)

"he obtained the promise," (vs.15) The word *promise* is the one that God gave Abraham after he had obeyed God by offering up Isaac (cf. James 2:21). Abraham was still trusting God to fulfil His former promise regarding his descendants by expecting Him to raise Isaac from the dead. (Gen. 22:16-17) Therefore, the author was calling his readers to do what God called Abraham to do when He instructed him to go to Mt. Moriah. He is urging them to continue trusting and obeying God despite going through persecutions. These Hebrew Christians needed to persevere. Having "patiently waited" and remained steadfast in the midst of difficulties. Abraham qualified to receive everything God wanted to give him. ("He obtained the promise"; cf. Col. 1:11; Heb. 12:1-3, 7; James 5:11)

"For men verily swear," (vs.16) But in swearing, one would appeal to someone greater than himself as confirmation of the truth of his statement. It is an argument from the less to the greater; if credit is given to man, who is by nature false, when he swears, and for this reason, because he confirms what he says by God's name, how much more credit is due to God, who is eternal truth, when he swears by himself? God in His sovereignty could appeal to no one greater since there is no one that is greater than Him. For instance, there are people that say, "I am telling the truth so help me God." Even God used "an oath" to guarantee His promise to bless Abraham greatly. (Gen. 22:16; cf. Exod. 32:13; Isa.45:23; Jer. 22:5; 49:13) "God [swearing] by Himself" signifies that He binds His word to His character. So, He swore by Himself in confirming the promise to Abraham. (Genesis 22:16ff)

"..the immutability of his counsel," (vs.17,18) However, the promises and the blessings of God to us are proved to be valid and sure by two immutable things: (1) God promised it, and God cannot lie. This was the assurance of the promise of the God who does not lie (Titus 1:2; Numbers 23:19; 1 Samuel 15:29); and (2) He confirmed the promise with an oath which was the assurance that God guaranteed it. Consequently, God gave Abraham double assurance that He would fulfil what He had promised him. Thus, the two unchangeable things are God's promise and His oath. God's doubly-strong

promise to Abraham, then, can be a "great (doubly-strong) encouragement" to us, now, because God has also promised us future blessings. God has promised that He we will give us rewards if we persevere faithfully now (cf. 2 Tim. 2:12) God indicated to those who would inherit the promise, that the promise was immutable, meaning it was unchangeable. He did not need affirmation to know if He would keep His promise because He does not lie. "God is not like the sons of men that he should lie and He is not like men that he should repent: has he then said, and shall he not do it? Has he spoken, and shall he not make it good?" (Numbers 23:19) The word of God, then, is a sure truth, and in itself authoritative, [αὐτόπιστος] self worthy of trust.

"Which hope we have," (vs.19) This sure promise becomes the basis of our hope, strong consolation and comfort. Our hope for the future is not based on some chance possibility, but on the sure promise and oath of God. This hope serves as an anchor to our soul. Therefore, we can be strong in confidence that we shall obtain what God has promised if we are faithful. (Hebrews 11:1; Romans 5:1,2; 8:24; Titus 1:2; Colossians 1:5; Hebrews 3:6; 7:19; 12:1) How can this serve as an anchor "which enters the Presence behind the veil"? The Presence behind the veil surely alludes to the Most Holy Place in the temple, where was located the Ark of the Covenant. The good illustration is that of an anchor, which sailors cast into the sea. Despite them not

seeing where the anchor takes hold in the depths they still trust it to take hold of some source of strength. They hold to that anchor by a strong rope or cable or chain. It then holds them so that wind, tide, and waves cannot cast them drifting to wreck on the rocks. That is how our hope in Christ is. Our hope is like that anchor for we hope for heaven where God dwells. Even so, we hold to the anchor of hope, trusting that it will keep us strong, so we can avoid the storms and winds of life that would destroy us.

"Whither the forerunner," (vs.20) In the illustration here, it is parallel to heaven, where Jesus went after He ascended. The author has now returned to the comparison of Jesus to Melchizedek. (5:10, 11) He now intends to continue the course of thought he had been on before he interrupted himself. These points will be discussed in more detail as the book progresses.

Hebrews 7

E. Jesus the Priest of Melchizedek's Order (7:1-28-8:6)

1. The facts of Melchizedek's significance (7:1-10)

(*a*) *Melchizedek's Priesthood was righteous and peaceful*
"*For this Melchizedek,*" (vs.1,2) The author now discusses the lesson concerning Melchizedek.And it was probably necessary that in him who was to be a type of the Son of God all things excellent should be found: and that Christ was shadowed forth by this type is evident from the Psalm referred to; for David did not say without reason, "Thou art a priest forever after the order Melchizedek;" To whom also Abraham gave a tenth part of all; first being by interpretation King of righteousness, and after that also King of Salem, which is, King of peace. The whole tribe of Levi was dedicated by God for His service (priesthood). All priests not only had to be Levites but also to be descended from Aaron and this priesthood was strictly national and Jewish.Melchizedek

was said to be king of Salem and priest of the Most High God, the true God, not an idol. Melchizedek means, in the original language, "king of righteousness." He is also called "king of Salem" (possibly a reference to Jerusalem, Psalm 76:2), and Salem means "peace." Therefore, Melchizedek was both king of righteousness and king of peace. Melchizedek was a type of Jesus Christ, since he is both King of both righteousness and peace. There was no permanent righteous or peace related to Aaronic priesthood. But Melchizedek was King of both righteousness and peace. Therefore having been justified (righteous) by faith we have peace with God through the Lord Jesus Christ. (Rom 5:1) Christ gives us peace and righteousness.

(b) Melchizedek's priesthood was personal not hereditary

"Without father, without mother," (vs.3) The author here actually implies that Melchizedek is like Christ in this. A person may be without offspring if he has no children but no one can be without parents and ancestors, without beginning of days or end of life. Melchizedek is said to have been without father, mother, and genealogy having neither beginning nor end. This does not mean that he came from nowhere, but nothing is recorded of his origin. The Levitical priesthood was hereditary. Melchizedek did not have these historical events in his life, but that they were irrelevant to his priestly office.

Just as he did not get his office from his parents nor did he pass it on to his offspring (whether or not he had them), so he did not receive his priesthood by virtue of his birth, nor did he pass it on to anyone at his death. He may have physically had beginning of days and end of life, even as Jesus did, but it was irrelevant to his priesthood. He was not born to be a priest, nor did anyone take his place as priest when he died. So his priestly office did not in any sense depend on his beginning of neither days nor end of life (as it did the Levitical priests). A man served as a priest not because of his right life, but because of his birth in the right family. In Aaronic priesthood genealogy was everything but in Melchizedek's priesthood, it was nothing. Melchizedek was a type of Christ because Jesus genealogy was not important in regard to His priesthood. The passage says Melchizedek was "made like unto the Son of God" as described. Without father, without mother, without descent, having neither beginning of days, nor end of life; but made like unto the Son of God; abideth a priest continually. In fact, this expression cannot be taken literally and physically regarding Jesus because he had a mother and beginning of days. These expressions are figurative and symbolic not physical and literal in such a way that some attempt to be highly physical. They conclude that Melchizedek must have appeared in the form of a man but that he was really supernatural.

(c) Melchizedek's priesthood was universal, not national

"But he whose descent is not counted from them," (vs.6) Levitical priests could minister only to Israel and only for Jehovah. But Melchizedek was a priest of the Most High God. (El-Elyon is universal name for God). The Most High God is over both Jew and Gentile and is first mentioned in the Bible in relation to Melchizedek. Jesus is not just the Messiah of Israel but of the world. His priesthood is universal just as Melchizedek.Priests under the Old Testament law had to be descendants of Aaron and had to be able to prove, by genealogy through their mother and father that they were qualified to serve as priests.

(d)Melchizedek's priesthood was Royal

"...the King of righteousness," (vs.2) The first likeness is in the name; for it was not without a mystery that he was called *the King of righteousness.* While this honor is ascribed to kings who rule with restraint and in justice, nevertheless, this is only referred to Christ. He not only exercises authority with justice as others kings do, but he also communicates to us the righteousness of God. Melchizedek himself was king. Any kind of rulership was totally foreign to the Levitical. The most significant point made both in Genesis 14 and in Psalms 110 is that Melchizedek was both king and priest at the same time.As other tribes, the Levites were subject to the king.

Their priestly functions were not under the control of the king, but in all other matters they were ordinary subjects. Melchizedek's priesthood and his royal office beautifully show Jesus savior hood and Lordship as a perfect king and perfect priest. The prophets in Israel had predicted the double role of priest king.

(e) Melchizedek's priesthood is eternal not temporary

"...having neither beginning of days," (vs.3) Melchizedek's priesthood had no time bounds. The priestly sacrifices by the high priest were not permanent. They had to be repeated and repeated. These sacrifices provided no permanent forgiveness or peace. The effects of sacrifices were temporary. Same was the time of priestly service. The author also points out the difference between Aaronic priests and Melchizedek priests in that Levitical priest were mortal men. They died and had to be replaced. This was not true of Melchizedek or of Christ. Again, as in verse 3, this could be meant figuratively referring only to the fact that no successor was ever named (despite the fact Melchizedek would have died). Again, the alternative meaning may be that Melchizedek actually was Jesus, so this applied to Him in that way too. Still another possibility is that Melchizedek was a man but never died, like Enoch and Elijah, who were just taken directly to heaven. This explains how he "lives," so is not "mortal." His ancestors and descendants don't matter, and his

successors did not exist. That is why nothing is told of them.

A priest served from the age of 25 years to 50 years. The order of priesthood in which he ministered was forever. This is a type of Christ's eternal priesthood. Jesus is a priest like Melchizedek whose priesthood is eternal.

(f) Abraham paid a tithe to Melchizedek

"..even the patriarch Abraham gave the tenth," (vs.4,5) Melchizedek was not a descendant of Abraham and was not even related to him, but yet Abraham paid tithes to him. If the Israelites paid tithes to the Levites and priests proved those priests were greater than the other Israelites, then Melchizedek who received tithe was greater than Abraham that paid it.And verily they that are of the sons of Levi, who receive the office of the priesthood, have a commandment to take tithes of the people according to the law, that is, of their brethren, though they come out of the loins of Abraham. Under the Old Covenant, Levites received tithes (Leviticus 27:30-33; Numbers 18:26-32; Deuteronomy 12:6, 17; 14:22-29; 26:12-15). All Hebrews agreed that their office made priests greater than other Israelites, even though all descended from Abraham. (They were greater in office and position, not necessarily in righteousness nor eternal reward, etc.) This shows that the Melchizedek order is superior to that of Aaron. Since

Jesus' priesthood was in the order of Melchizedek, his priesthood is then superior to that of the Old Covenant.

(g) Melchizedek blessed Abraham

"...the less is blessed of the better," (vs.6-8) The author continues showing the greatness of Melchizedek by stating that he blessed Abraham, not the other way around. Abraham who had the promises from God was blessed by Melchizedek. He states that everyone knows that the one who is greater in office or position blesses the one who is lesser, not the other way around (Genesis 27:27ff; Luke 24:50f; and 47:10). This also is a clear sign that since Abraham paid tithe to Melchizedek, Melchizedek was greater than Abraham.

(h) Levi paid tithes to Melchizedek

"Levi also, who receiveth tithes, payed tithes in Abraham," (vs.9, 10) The sense is that, if Abraham paid tithes to Melchizedek, then in a figurative language, Levi paid tithes to Melchizedek. This, in turn, means that the Melchizedek order of priesthood is greater than that of Levi. Levi also, who receiveth tithes, paid tithes in Abraham. Since, Levi was still in the loins of his father when Melchizedek met Abraham he also paid tithe to Melchizedek.The author seems to be dealing with types, comparisons because how can Levi pay tithes when he is only in the loins of his father? At that time, Levi was a numerous generations after Abraham. The means that,

Levi received his position of honour because of being a descendant of Abraham to whom the promises referred to in chapter 6 had been made. Therefore, if Melchizedek was greater than Abraham, then logically the same thing must apply to Levi, who could not possibly be greater than Abraham.

2. The change of priesthood (7:11-19)

(a) The deficiency in the Old Covenant priesthood

"If therefore perfection were by the Levitical priesthood," (vs.11) The author shows that there was something lacking in the Old Covenant priesthood of Levi. This is proved by the fact that another priest was prophesied to come after a different order of priest. If all the needs of the people were perfectly met by the Levitical priesthood, why would God ever prophesy a priest of a different order? The term "Perfect" here, as in 2:10 and 5:9, has nothing to do with sinlessness or righteousness. The author is not implying that Levitical priesthood was sinful or wicked. It is also not implying that it could not achieve the purpose for which God had given it. The Old Covenant achieved what God gave it for though its purpose was temporary. The Old Covenant and its Levitical priesthood were not "perfect" in the sense that men have needs regarding salvation which that system could not fill. (10:1-18) The old covenant was abrogated by the coming of Christ. However, a system was very much in need in order to "perfect" what was

lacking. The author tells us that the people received the law under the Levitical priesthood. The change of priesthood required the change of law. The law was given by Moses through His spokesman Aaron the high priest. It was then taught to the people by the priests. The ceremonies and rituals of that law were administered for the people by the priests. If the priesthood changed, it must be because the law itself changed.

The author is saying that in fact you no longer may choose the Old Covenant and still please God, for God Himself has chosen to remove that law. This is a major development in the teaching of the book. Psalms 110 was a confirmation that there would be a change in the priesthood which also meant change of the law.

"..pertaineth to another tribe," (vs.13) Jewish students often misunderstood David's prophecies, yet they all knew that he did often prophesy regarding his offspring the Messiah. (Matthew 22:41 and Acts 2:25) However, admitting this fact meant admitting to all what the author was saying since they knew that David was of the tribe of Judah and so the Messiah, David's rightful heir to the throne, must also be of the tribe of Judah. But priests were of the tribe of Levi and nothing anywhere in the writings of Moses allowed priests to serve of the tribe of Judah. If really the Messiah was a priest despite the fact He could not serve as priest under the law, then the law must have changed.

"which tribe Moses spake nothing concerning priesthood," (vs.14) The author says that Moses by no means said anything that allowed priests to be of the tribe of Judah. That means that under the law, it was wrong for one from the tribe of Judah to serve as priest. Some Scriptures teach (Like Hezekiah) that kings could not offer sacrifices. However, these are not the arguments made here by the author. It is enough to know that God specified one tribe and never said people of the other tribes could do the job.

(b) A priest after the order of Melchizedek

"..there ariseth another priest, "(vs.15)The statement was that there would be another priest, not after the order of Aaron, with its emphasis on the flesh, but after the order of Melchizedek. Priests after the order of Aaron had many other physical qualifications needed and physical rituals celebrated. But there is no indication of such regarding Melchizedek, or regarding Christ. Our High Priest Jesus was promised in Psalms 110 to be a priest forever. He serves by the power of an endless life. He needs no replacement, so no need for emphasis on physical ancestry. Since Christ would be of a tribe of Judah and not from the Levitical priests, is one proof that He must serve under a different law.

Just as Jesus Christ, Melchizedek was priest and king at the same time. This was impossible under the Law of Moses because these two offices were received by physical inheritance through two separate tribes. Kings were descendants of David of the tribe of Judah, and priests were descendants of Aaron of the tribe of Levi. No one man could ever, therefore, serve in both capacities under the law.

The prophecy of Psalms 110 (Read Zechariah 6:12f) prove that the Messiah would be both priest and king. This not only proves a change of the law, it also proves that, when Jesus is priest, He will also be king. He was to be priest and king at the same time. If He is not now priest, then He cannot have offered sacrifice for our sins.

(c) A disannulling of the commandment (Vs, 18)

This does not say the law was sinful or evil or that God made a mistake in giving it but it simply means it was never designed to fully meet man's need for salvation from sin. It was designed to prepare us for the better system of the gospel (Galatians 3:19-25) and absolutely did its work. But it could never permanently forgive sin (chapter 10) and could not make people perfect as regards righteousness before God. It was weak and unprofitable in meeting that need of mankind (Romans 8:3; Galatians 2:16; Acts 13:39). The figure of the whole is that the ministry of Moses was no less temporary than that of Aaron; and so both were annulled by the coming of Christ, for the one could not stand without the other. By the word *Law*, we mean what peculiarly belonged to Moses; for the Law contains the rule of life and the unjustified covenant of life; and in it we find everywhere many remarkable sentences by which we are instructed as to faith, and as to the fear of God. None of these were abolished by Christ, but only that part which regarded the ancient priesthood. Since we clearly need forgiveness, the law had to be replaced. The former command was annulled and a better hope of the gospel was offered which leads to eternal life. If sin is not forgiven, we remain enemies of god and once sin has been forgiven, we can again approach God in harmony and fellowship. The point then is that the Hebrew Christians must not go back to the Old Covenant because it is not just inferior but is totally abrogated and no longer stands in effect. The Old Covenant can no longer serve us at all because for God no longer recognizes it as being in force! Verses 12 and 18 are the first of many statements in Hebrews that the law is just no longer in effect.

3. Jesus Christ the Priest Forever (7:20-28)

(a) The surety of a better Testament (VV 20-22)

*"And inasmuch as not without an oath he was made priest.., "*Just as God had made the promise to Abraham with an oath to confirm it (6:13ff), so He confirmed with an oath His promise to make Christ a priest forever after the order of Melchizedek. This was not true of Levitical priests who were made priests by the law without an Oath of God. But God's oath shows the sureness of this priesthood of Jesus and also the importance of it. (Read

6:13ff.) The New Covenant is better than the Old Covenant for because our High Priest is greater than the Old Covenant priests. Since we have a better priesthood, we should stay with the New Covenant.

Priesthood was necessary to God's provision for forgiveness, worship, and teaching. It was so essential to the provisions of the system that, if we now have a better priesthood, then we have a better system. Christ is the "surety" of a better covenant. "Surety" is like bail money which guarantees that a person will show up for his trial. It is the personal guarantee that something is valid, real, or will really work. So the guarantee to us that the New Covenant is better than the Old Testament is that Jesus Himself is our High Priest. In fact, He is the whole sum and substance of what the covenant is about. Without Him, the New Covenant would be no better than the Old. With Him, we have assurance that our system is better. The new covenant is better than the old. This is one of many "better" statements in Hebrews showing that the new is better than the old. This is the reason why the author is encouraging these Hebrew Christians not to leave the New to go back to the old.

This is the first use of the word "Testament" or "Covenant" in the book of Hebrews, yet it will be used many more times. This word means an arrangement or system, especially a system for providing blessings or property. The word can refer to an agreement between two parties, but the word itself does not always require that both parties agree to the terms. It can refer to the terms of a "last will and testament," but again it does not inherently require that the giver die. It is an agreement devised by one who seeks to dispense something to others. This is the system by which God determines who will receive His blessings for men, especially the blessing of forgiveness and the resulting favour of God.

(b) The unchangeable priesthood (VV 23, 24)

The priests under the Old Covenant would serve a while, and then die. *"And they truly were many priests, because they were not suffered to continue by reason of death: But this man, because he continueth ever, hath an unchangeable priesthood."* Then another priest had to be appointed, learning the job and its duties by experience over time. Thus priests were repeatedly being replaced. Jesus our High Priest lives forever serving without end and as our perfect High Priest, will never be replaced.

(c) Jesus our All-Sufficient Intercessor (vs. 25)

In what sense can Jesus save to the uttermost? *Wherefore he is able also to save them to the uttermost that comes unto God by him, seeing he ever liveth to make intercession for them.* There is no sin He cannot forgive if we truly repent of it – 1 John 1:7, 9. Further, these sins, once forgiven, are *completely removed*, never to be held against us again. (10:17) They are remembered no more. He can save *all people* of every race, nationality, or gender. Truly, Jesus can save to the uttermost. Old

Covenant priests could not save anyone. But Jesus can save any and all, no matter what sins we have committed. And this will always be true because He will always live to "intercede" for us. To "intercede" is to serve as an advocate or to plead to one person on behalf of another person. Jesus goes to God on our behalf, offering His sacrifice for us, just as Old Covenant priests did. Further, the passage shows that salvation is only through Jesus. He is the High Priest; therefore we must approach God through Him. He is the sacrifice, so we must receive the forgiveness He offers. No one else can save us from our sins. (Acts 4:12; John 14:6)

(d) Jesus the Great Sacrifice (VV 26-28)

Jesus gave Himself *"once for all,"* unlike those Old Testament priests that had to give sacrifices "daily." This too will be discussed further later. The Old Testament priests offered yearly sacrifices, monthly sacrifices, weekly sacrifices, daily sacrifices, and other sacrifices anytime someone sinned. But it had to be done again and again because no one sacrifice could take care of all sins for all people for all time. For such an high priest became us, who is holy, harmless, undefiled, separate from sinners, and made higher than the heavens; Who needeth not daily, as those high priests, to offer up sacrifice, first for his own sins, and then for the people's: for this he did once, when he offered up himself. For the law maketh men high priests which have infirmity; but the word of the oath, which was since the law, maketh the Son, who is consecrated for evermore.Jesus is more suitable as our priest than the Old Covenant priests because He is sinless. The Old Covenant priests had to offer sacrifices for their own sins, as well as the sins of the people. (5:3 and 9:7; Leviticus 16:11-15) They were sinners themselves, so their sacrifices were for their own benefit as well as the benefit of the people. But Jesus Christ who was priest according to an oath, not according to the law (7:20-22), has no such sins or weaknesses. Our High priest is perfectly sinless and now is perfected to meet all our needs.

He is never deceitful, never seeks to hurt us, but always serves for our benefits. But the Old Covenant priests sometimes used their authority selfishly and sinfully, taking advantage of the people. Old Testament prophets repeatedly had to be rebuked for such selfish conducts. (1 Samuel 2, 3)

- Jesus is *undefiled*, pure and sinless that no sin has ever defiled His character. Under the law, if a priest was defiled (as by an unclean body), he could not serve as priest. Imagine our condition if, even for a short time, Jesus could not serve as our priest because He had disqualified Himself by some improper conduct. We need not be concerned, however, for our High Priest is undefiled.

- He lived a life *separate from sinners* in that, though He lived around them and tried to help them, yet He was never so influenced by them as to partake of their evils. Surely if our High Priest was so holy and separated from sinners, we should imitate His example and keep ourselves pure.

- Jesus was made *higher than the heavens* (Ephesians 4:10). He was exalted to the highest position anyone could be in heaven as a result of His faithful service here. (Philippians 2:9-11; Ephesians 1:19-23)

Hebrews 8

4. Our High Priest Ministers in Heaven (8:1-6)

The author first stated (vv. 1-2), and then explained (vv. 3-5), Jesus better ministry which is better than the Old Covenant priesthood in three ways: (i) He serves as a seated priest, having finished His work of offering a final sacrifice for sins. (v. 1) (ii) He is an enthroned priest, having taken His place at the right hand of God the Father. (v. 1) And (iii) He is a heavenly priest, having entered the true sanctuary where He now ministers. (vv. 1-2)

"Now of the things," (vs.1) The author now introduced this admonition, that he might keep his hearers attentive to what he had in view. He is showing that Jesus is a high priest whose ministry is in heaven. Therefore, the priesthood established by Moses under the law was made void, for it was earthly. Jesus suffered in the flesh and having taken the form of a servant he made himself of no reputation in the world. (Philippians 2:7) He further reminds us of his ascension unto the right hand of the throne of God, for it is through the power of the Spirit which gloriously appeared in the resurrection and the ascension of Christ, that the dignity of his priesthood is to be anticipated.

Having proved the superiority of Christ to all the mediators of the Old Covenant (better than prophets, angels, Moses, Joshua and Aaron), a priest after a different order, the author shows that Christ is the minister of the true tabernacle. He now shows that the priesthood of Christ is the main point of what He has been saying.

The phrase *"of the sanctuary"* or literally *"of holy things"*(vs.2) This should be taken as being in the neuter gender which the author explains it as, *"of the true tabernacle."*"True" literally means "genuine." or real" – not as opposed to that which is false, but as compared with the tabernacle in the wilderness which was a mere copy. "The law was given by Moses, but grace and truth came by Jesus Christ." Then the old tabernacle was not the empty inventions of man, but the copy of the heavenly tabernacle. A "copy" or "shadow" is significant in at least the following ways: (1) Shadows can prove the real thing exists and is coming. (2) Copies or shadows tell, at least in general or outline form, what the real thing is like. (3) Yet, we ought to prefer to real thing over the copy or shadow. This means that the Hebrews had the copy of good things under the Old Covenant. Now they have the real thing. Why go back? The tabernacle built by Moses was not a false one, and was not an invention of man but the model of the heavenly tabernacle. The author denies it to have been the true tabernacle but a shadow, for a shadow differs from the substance, and the sign from the thing signified. It is better to take "holy things" as designating the holy ministries of the priest, afterwards specified when the offering of gifts and sacrifices is mentioned, than as signifying "the sanctuary." He again referred to "the heavens," where Jesus Christ now serves as High Priest in the "real (true) tabernacle." "The throne that Jesus occupies and from which He ministers is not the throne of David which He will one day occupy here on earth as the promised Messiah. (Matt. 25:31) Our High Priest was identified with the throne of 'the Majesty in the heavens.Christ is a priest and a minister in holy things, and a minister in the true tabernacle. He is the mediator of a better covenant established on better promises

"Which the Lord pitched, "For doubtless he suffered on earth, and by an earthly blood he atoned for our sins, for he derived his origin from the seed of Abraham; the sacrifice of his death was visible; and lastly, that he might offer himself to the Father, it was necessary for him to descend from heaven to the earth, and as man to become exposed to the sorrows of this mortal life, and at length to death itself. To all this I reply, that whatever of an earthly kind appears at first sight to be in Christ, it is to be viewed spiritually by the eye of faith. Thus his flesh, which proceeded from the seed of Abraham, since it was the temple of God, possessed a vivifying power; yea, the death of Christ became the life of the world, which is certainly above nature.

The phrase *"For every high priest,"* (vs.3) shows that Christ's priesthood cannot coexist with the Levitical priesthood. He proves that Christ had no sacrifice, such as was offered under the Law; it hence follows, that his priesthood is not earthly or carnal, but one of a more excellent character."The author asserts that the gift and sacrifice which Christ offered was Himself (5:1 compared to 8:3) and that he has achieved what the sacrificial action of the high priest on the Day of Atonement only foreshadowed. His entrance into the heavenly sanctuary demonstrates the superiority of his priestly service to the ministry of the O.T priesthood.

The phrase *"For if he were on earth,"*(vs.4) means that Christ is a high priest; but as the office of a judge does not exist without laws and statutes, so the office of sacrificing must be connected with Christ as a priest: yet he has no earthly or visible sacrifice; he cannot then be a priest on earth. We must always hold this truth that when he speaks of the death of Christ, he regards not the external action, but the spiritual benefit. He suffered death as men do, but as a priest he atoned for the sins of the world in a divine manner; there an external shedding of blood, but there was also an internal and spiritual purgation; in a word, he died on earth, but the virtue and efficacy of his death proceeded from heaven.

"..example or copy, and shadow."(vs.5) the earthly tabernacle was a copy of a heavenly reality, emblem of a spiritual, heavenly sanctuary. The phrase "But now"

means "as the case now stands."A New Covenant
implies a new ministry; a better covenant implies a better
ministry. Christ's priesthood implies a sanctuary. The
new sanctuary implies a New Covenant. The phrase
"Who serve unto the example" is the Greek verb
[λατρεύειν] "to serve," which means the performing of
sacred rites; and so [ἐν] or [ἐπὶ] is to be understood
correctly. This is certainly more appropriate than the
rendering given by some, "Who serve the shadow and
example of heavenly things." In short, he teaches us that
the true worship of God consists not in the ceremonies of
the Law, and that hence the Levitical priests, while
exercising their functions, had nothing but a shadow and
a copy, which is inferior to the prototype, for this is the
meaning of the word [ὑποδείγμα], exemplar. *The phrase
"As Moses was admonished of God,"* is found in Exodus
25:40; and the author explains that the ministry
according to the Law, was a picture as it was intended to
be a shadow of what was to be found in Jesus Christ.
God commanded that all the parts of the tabernacle
should match with the original pattern, which he had
shown Moses on the mountain. "Probably the conception
of the tabhanith, the 'model' (Exodus 25:9), also goes
back ultimately to the idea that the earthly sanctuary is
the counterpart of the heavenly dwelling of a deity [in
ancient Near Eastern thought]."[8] This is a remarkable

---

[8]Frank M. Cross, "The Tabernacle," Biblical Archaeologist 10:3
(September 1947):62. Cf.

passage, for it contains three things entitled to special notice. The Old Covenant with Israel had Moses and Prophets as the mediators. But they were not real mediators, only reflections of the true mediator who was to come. The New Covenant not only has a better mediator and better promises. The phrase *"But now has he obtained a more excellent ministry,"* (vs.6) means that Christ's priesthood is more excellent than that of Aaron, because he is the interpreter and Mediator of a better covenant. All covenants are based on promises. Concerning God's covenants it is always His promises that are imperative for men break their promises but God does not. The author says now that it was but right that Moses and Aaron should give way to Christ as to one more excellent, because the gospel is a more excellent covenant than the Law, and also because the death of Christ was a nobler sacrifice than the victims under the Law.Jesus could not have been a priest during His lifetime on earth, because the law already provided for priests of a different order, different tribe, etc. The author puts this in the presence tense, not because the law was still in effect – he is about to prove and has already stated that the law had been disannulled – but because the priests were continuing their ritualistic service even in his day. This continued till the Romans destroyed the temple in Jerusalem in AD 70. Those priests would surely never have allowed one of the tribe of Judah to offer sacrifice (and, of course, there is no reason for animal sacrifice in the temple anymore, anyway).

III. The Superiority of the New Covenant (8:7-10:18)

A. Old Covenant to be replaced by the new (8:7-13)

The phrase *"For if that first covenant had been faultless,"* (vs.7) Another Covenant has been substituted and from this it is clear that the old covenant was not in every respect perfect. To establish this he adduces the testimony of Jeremiah. In the quotations from Jeremiah 31:31-34 are eight factors which show that the New Covenant is superior to the old: (i) It was written by God; (ii) The covenant in Christ is new and is better than the old; (iii) God has never made a covenant with Gentiles. Therefore, the New Covenant also is made with the same people of Israel. Gentiles can be beneficiaries of the New Covenant as they could be of the old. God said to Abraham "All the nations shall be blessed in you". This covenant is fulfilled in each of us when we accepted Jesus as our Lord; (iv) The blessings of the Old Covenant were conditioned on people's obedience to the Law. The New Covenant is not so. It is based on the Love of God through the finished work of Jesus on the Cross. It is none of our doing but just the grace of God upon us; (v) everything under the old covenant was external; obedience was primarily out of fear. Under the new it is to be out of love and thanksgiving. In the new covenant true worship is internal, not ritual; (vi) Being internal, the New Covenant has to be personal. God's spirit is within us to teach us all things; (vii) Under Old Covenant sins could never be forgotten because they were never really forgiven. They were only covered. In the New Covenant God forgets every sin; and (viii) Christ's unique sacrifice was finished with the result that all men in Christ had access to God. The age of Moses' Law was over and now the age of the son was come forever. Hebrews eight and six is a very important verse. It connects two major arguments in the epistle. The first argument (1:1-8:6) proves Christ to be the better mediator. The second argument proves the New Covenant mediated by the blood covenant. (8:6) The first covenant is described in Exodus 20. The basis of the New Covenant is the promise of God- "I will." (Jeremiah 31:31-34) The benefit of the New Covenant rests upon the pledged assurance of God`s Grace. The first covenant was faulty and imperfect. (7:19; 8:7) While the first covenant was still in force, a search for a second covenant was going on. (Jeremiah 31:31-34; Hebrews 8:8-12) It did not enable the people to line up to its just demands. The blood sacrifices did not take sin that hindered man from approaching God. The entire Leviticus system served its purpose as a school master to bring man to Christ. (It was pointing to Christ). "Them," signifies the possessors of the first covenant.

The phrase *"Behold, the days come,"* (vs.8) speaks of future time; he arraigns the people of disloyalty, because they continued not faithful after having received the Law. The Law, then, was the covenant which was broken, as God complains, by the people. To remedy this evil, he promised a new and a different covenant, the fulfillment of which prophecy was the abrogation of the old covenant. (Jeremiah 31:31-34) By the days which the prophet mentions, all agree that Christ's kingdom is signified; it hence follows, that the old covenant was changed by the coming of Christ. And he names *the house of Israel and the house of Judah,* because the posterity of Abraham had been divided into two kingdoms. So the promise is to gather again all the elect together into one body. God who made the first covenant with Israel will also make the New Covenant with His people. (House of Israel and house of Judah but those who believe in Christ into the blessings of the covenant) God makes no covenant with the Gentiles.

"Not according to the covenant" (vs.9) is expressing the difference between the covenant which then existed and the new one which he caused them to expect. The Prophet now explicitly declares that it would be one unlike the former. By saying that the covenant was made in the day when he laid hold on their hand to rescue them from bondage, he enhanced the sin of defection by thus reminding them of so great a benefit. At the same time he did not accuse one age only of ingratitude; but as these very men who had been delivered immediately fell away, and as their posterity after their example continually relapsed, hence the whole nation had become covenant breakers. When Israel was a child, a minor, and Jehovah took them by the hand, He placed them under Laws and regulations. (Galatians 4:1-2) The first was temporary, beginning at Sinai up to Calvary. (Romans 10:4).The second is eternal, an everlasting covenant (Hebrews 13:20) In the first covenant, a covenant of works, its fulfillment depended upon the works of the creature. In the better covenant God is bound by word, and oath to the doing of His own good pleasure in accomplishing the whole work of His people's peace. In the Old Covenant were words like, "thou shall" and "thou shall not" but in the New Covenant are words like, "I will" and "I will not." Verse 10-12; give us a description of the New Covenant. (2 Corinthians 3:3) People are to be possessed by God as His own people.

"For this is the covenant that I will make," (vs. 10) describes three main parts in this covenant; the first regards the unjustified remission of sins; and the other, the inward renovation of the heart; there is a third which depends on the second, and that is the illumination of the mind as to the knowledge of God. There are here many things most deserving of notice. The first is that God calls us to himself without effect as long as he speaks to us in no other way than by the voice of man. He indeed teaches us and commands what is right but he speaks to the deaf; for when we seem to hear anything, our ears are only struck by an empty sound; and the heart, full of depravity and perverseness rejects every wholesome doctrine. In short, the word of God never penetrates into our hearts, for they are iron and stone until they are softened by him; nay, they have engraven on them a contrary law, for perverse passions rule within, which lead us to rebellion. In vain then does God proclaim his Law by the voice of man, unless he writes it by his Spirit on our hearts, that is, unless he forms and prepares us for obedience. It hence appears of what avail is freewill and the uprightness of nature before God regenerates us. The second particular refers to the gratuitous pardon of sins. Though they have sinned, saith the Lord, yet I will pardon them. This part is also most necessary; for God never so forms us for obedience to his righteousness, but that many corrupt affections of the flesh still remain; nay, it is only in part that the viciousness of our nature is

corrected; so that evil lusts break out now and then. And hence is that contest of which Paul complains, when the godly do not obey God as they ought, but in various ways offend. (Romans 7:13) Whatever desire then there may be in us to live righteously, we are still guilty of eternal death before God, because our life is ever very far from the perfection which the Law requires. There would then be no stability in the covenant, except God gratuitously forgave our sins. But it is the peculiar privilege of the faithful who have once embraced the covenant offered to them in Christ, that they feel assured that God is propitious to them; nor is the sin to which they are liable, a hindrance to them, for they have the promise of pardon. *"And they shall be to mea people,* "speaks of the fruit of the covenant, that God chooses us for his people, and assures us that he will be the guardian of our salvation. This is indeed the meaning of these words, *"And I will be to them a God;"* for he is not the God of the dead, nor does he take us under his protection, but that he may make us partakers of righteousness and of life, so that David justly exclaims, "Blessed are the people to whom the Lord is God (Psalm 144:15), we see that under the Old Covenant Israel was Ignorant of God (Isaiah 1).Under the New Covenant, Israel shall know the Lord. *I will put my laws in their mind*; for it is the work of the Spirit of God to illuminate our minds, so that we may know what the will of God is, and also to bend our hearts to obedience. Therefore, to attain it no one is able except through the secret revelation of the Spirit.

"And they shall not teach every man his neighbor," (vs.11) Hence Isaiah, in speaking of the restoration of the Church, saying that all God's children would be his disciples or scholars. (Isaiah 28:16) The meaning is the same when he introduces God as saying, *they shall know me.* For God does not promise what is in our own power, but what he alone can perform for us. In the first instance, "know" is the word used where one commends God to the knowledge of one who is ignorant of him. The second translation, "know" speaks of an absolute acquaintance. Under the first covenant, there was remembrance of sins every year by reason of constant repetition of sacrifices; (Hebrews 10:3,4) under the New Covenant, sins are forgotten because they are put away by the final sacrifice which has paid for all sins. (Jeremiah 31:31). the first covenant was made "Old" six hundred years before Calvary, even in Jeremiah's day. "Old" means that which is worn out. Out molded and outputted not in point of time.

In Verse 13, *the phrase "In that he saith, A new,"* means that as one covenant was being established, he infers the subversion of the other; and by calling it the old covenant, he assumes that it was to be abrogated; for what is old tends to decay. Besides, as the new is substituted, it must be that the former has come to an end; for the second, as it has been said, is of another character. But if the whole dispensation of Moses, as far as it was opposed to the dispensation of Christ, has passed away, then the ceremonies also must have ceased. The Four things provided in the New Covenant are that; the Law will no more be merely external, but a law written in the heart, the people are to be possessed by God as His own People, the people will be on intimate and affectionate conditions with God so that the knowledge of God will be general, Sin will be dealt with once for all, and there shall be entire forgiveness of sins.

Hebrews 9

B. The Symbolic Sanctuary (9:1-10)

1. Articles of the tabernacle (9:1-5)

"..of divine service, and a worldly sanctuary," (vs.1)
That tabernacle was divided into two parts, the Holy
Place (sanctuary) and the Most Holy Place or Holy of
Holies. Jesus' priesthood mediates a better covenant
(8:7-13), so he mediates in a better sanctuary. The law
was their school master (Galatians 3:24), teaching by
types and shadows, which served as objects and lessons
to point them to Messiah. *The phrase "Then verily the
first,"*[9] speaks generally of the abrogation of the old
covenant, he now refers specially to the ceremonies. His
object is to show that there was nothing practiced then to
which Christ's coming has not put an end. He says first,
that under the old covenant there was a specific form of
divine worship, and that it was markedly adapted to that
time. The sense is that the whole form or manner of
worshipping God was annexed to the old covenant and
that it consisted of sacrifices, ablutions, and other

---

9 Rather, "Yet even the first," etc. It is connected with the last verse
of the preceding chapter; as though he had said, — "Though the
covenant is become antiquated, yet it had many things divinely
appointed connected with it." Mèv oὖv mean "yet," or however. See
Art. 8:4. Macknight has "Now verily;" and Stuart, "Moreover."

symbols, together with the sanctuary. And he calls it a *worldly sanctuary*. Hence the sanctuary in itself was indeed *worldly*, and is rightly classed among the elements of the world; it was yet heavenly as to what it signified. When the Messiah, the Antitype and Fulfiller of all types and prophecies, had come, the Old Covenant had served its purpose, types give way to the Antitype, shadows give way to substance, and pictures give way to Reality. The *worldly sanctuary* is no longer required. Israel looked upon the tabernacle as most sacred for in it was the presence of God (Shekinah glory) which meant that God`s presence was in the midst of His People. (Exodus 25:8) The meaning of "Worldly" is literally" of his world." the holy place was in the world. This signifies it to be visible, tangible, built with earthly materials. (Galatians 4:3; Colossians 2:20) It was built according to the patterns shown to Moses on the mount (8:5) Exodus 23:33-35.The sanctuary had ordinances of divine services and was appointment of God, (Tabernacle, literally, a tent) the word "Tabernacle" is found ten times in the epistle, but the word "temple" is not mentioned.

The three articles of furniture in the Tabernacle in the holy place were;

(a) The Candlestick (better translated the Lamp stand)

The Lamp stand [shemeshi] in Hebrew was set at the door of the tabernacle from the east, the seven branched golden candlestick was at the left, on the south side of the room. There were no windows in the tabernacle because natural light cannot reveal spiritual truths. (Exodus 25:31-40; 37:17-24) The seven lamps constantly fed by oil represented the fullness of light that is in Christ Jesus. Psalm 45:7, John 3:34 Act 2:33.We receives the light of revelation truth through the word. We receive by inward and supernatural illumination.

(b) The table and the showbread

This was set on the north side of the room, apposite the candlestick. (Exodus 25:23-30; 37:10; Leviticus 24:5-9) The table speaks of communion and fellowship (2 Samuel 9), illustrates God`s grace in Christ. Just as David showed kindness to Mephibosheth for Jonathan's sake, so God shows kindness toward us for Jesus Christ`s sake. Jesus is the true bread. (John 6:32) The word "Showbread: is literally "bread of faces" or "bread of presence." (Exodus25:10) There were also 12 loaves that represented 12 tribes of Israel before God, Like the 12 precious stones in the High Priest`s breastplate. The third piece of furniture is not mentioned here:

(c) The Golden Censer

A veil separated the Holy Place from the Most Holy Place or Holiest of All (Exodus 26:31-33). This Most Holy Place had the golden censer (NKJV and KJV) or the golden altar of incense (ASV, NASB, and RSV). This is confusing because other descriptions place the golden altar outside the Most Holy Place in the Holy Place. (Exodus 30:1-6; 37:25f; etc.) Two possible explanations are: (1) The verse does not technically say the altar was *in* the Most Holy Place but that the Most Holy Place "*had*" the golden altar. (Exodus 40:5; 30:6; 1 Kings 6:22) The altar was just outside the veil and its service pertained to the significance of the Most Holy Place in that it was used to offer sacrifice on the Day of Atonement, the day when the high priest took animal blood into the Most Holy Place. (Exodus 30:1-10) (2) It is uncertain whether the proper translation is to refer to the golden altar of incense or to a golden censer used in burning incense in the Most Holy Place. (Leviticus 15:12) See notes above regarding translations. This was the article of furniture which was found in the holiest place. (Vs 2) When speaking of the articles of furniture in the holy place the author omitted the altar of incense which stood before the veil separating the holy of holies from the rest of the tabernacle. (Exodus 30:6, 1-6) This golden censer full of burning coals of fire was carried into the Holy of Holies by the High Priest on the Day of Atonement. (Leviticus 16:12, 13) The incense was then put upon the fire and the cloud of the incense covered the mercy seat. Thus, the golden censer had to do with the holy of holies, but was not a permanent article of furniture contained in it.

(d)The Ark of the Covenant

The term "ark" means simply box or chest. It was 54 inches long, 27 inches wide and about 27 inches high. (Exodus 25:10-22) The ark, with the mercy seat, which formed its lid or cover, was the only piece of furniture in the Holy of Holies. The ark was the symbol of God's presence and of his covenant blessing resting upon His people. The wood was overlaid with God, prefiguring Christ's divine glory. It was made of shutting wood, which never rotted. (Incorruptible wood- Septuagint translation of O.T) The wood and Gold symbolized the two natures in the God- man. the ark formed God's throne in Israel. (Psalm 80:1) The pot of manna and Aaron's rod were not kept in the ark in Solomon's day when it contained nothing but the tables of the law. (1 Kings 8:9; 2, Chronicles 5:10, Exodus 16:33, Numbers 17:10) Aaron's rod that budded and yielded almonds (Numbers 17:8, Chronicles 16) is the lifeless rod being made to blossom. It is a figure of the resurrected Christ. The Ark of the Covenant (Deut 10:1-5) foreshadows the Christ who magnified the laws in His life and in His death. (Isaiah 42:21; Psalm 40:7, 8; Galatians 4:4; Matthew 5:17, Romans 5:19, Isaiah 45:24).The lid of the ark which formed the covering was called the mercy seat. it was the form of a cherubim with outreached wings, which wings met at the centre thus overshadowing as it were protecting God's throne. (Ex 25:17-22) The Cherubims are associated with the administration of God's judicial authority. (Gen 3:24;

Rev 4:6-8, Ezekiel 1:5-10) The Shekinah of God's presence abode between the Cherubims on the Mercy Seat. The word "Mercy Seat" is translated "propitiation." (Romans 3:25; Luke 18:13)

2. Sacrifices and Rituals in the Tabernacle (9:6-10)

The author had introduced the tabernacle, not to discuss its furnishings in detail, but to make a point about the sacrifices offered there by the priests. *"Now, when these things were thus ordained,"*(vs.6) Omitting other things, he undertakes to handle the main point in dispute: he says that the priests who performed sacred rites were to enter the first tabernacle daily, but that the High Priest entered the holy of holies only yearly with the appointed sacrifice. The author next explains some of the symbolic meaning of this. We will see that the Most Holy Place represents heaven, and the high priest going into it to make atonement for the people represents Jesus' going to heaven to present to God His blood as atonement for our sins. (9:24) *"accomplishing the service of God,"* (vs.6) The priests would perform services regularly in the first part of the tabernacle, the Holy Place.

"But into the second went." (vs.7) But only the high priest went into the Most Holy Place, and he did that one time a year on the Day of Atonement to offer sacrifice for his own sins and those of the people. (Leviticus 16:1-34; 23:26-32; Exodus 30:10; Numbers 29:7-11) (He actually entered the Most Holy Place several times on each Day of Atonement, but that day came only once a

year) The Leviticus Priesthood is temporary (Hebrews 9:6-10). Priests were restricted from going into the holy of holies. Their services were a sacred one. It was a daily repetition consisting of:

a) Dressing the lamps of the candlestick.

Supplying holy oil and trimming their wicks. This was done every evening and morning.

b) Burning incense every day at the altar of incense.

This was done immediately after the offering of the evening and morning sacrifices. While this service was being performed, people were praying outside (Luke 1:10).

c) Changing the Showbread on the table.

This was done every Sabbath morning, on the tenth day of the seventh month (corresponds to our September) Israel`s High Priest entered the holy of holies to present the blood of propitiatory sacrifices before the Lord (Lev 16:4; Ex 28:2). He entered the most holy place at least three times in his very day.

First: - He entered the sacred place carrying a censer full of burning coals and with his hands full of incense which he placed upon the coals so that the cloud of incense should cover the Mercy Seat. (Lev 16:12)

Second: - He took the blood of the bullock, which had been killed for a sin offering, for himself and his house. (Lev 16:14)

Third: - He went out and killed the goat, which was the sin offering for the people, and did with its blood as he had done with that of the bullock (Lev 16:15).

The phrase *"once every year"* Foreshadowed the fact that Christ entered heaven "once for all" (9:12).

The word "errors" refers to sins of ignorance. (Read Lev 4:2; 5:15; Number 15:22; Psalm 19:13; Heb 10:28; Psalm 51:1-3; 16, 17) The word translated "figure" is not the same meaning as type in Rom 5:14; 1 Corinthians 10:6, but is the same as that translated "parable" as in Matthews 13:3. A parable was an object lesson as long as it was in use, and thus pointed to the actual tabernacle, which was not yet in use.

The "Gift" refers to general offerings, such as the meal offering, oil, frankincense and salt which were mingled there with (Lev 2), the first fruit, tithes and all free will offerings.

The "sacrifices" have reference to the blood sacrifices. (Lev 1:2, 3, 10) The word *"perfect"* does not mean sinless, but complete, finished. It means to complete or equip. The gifts and services of the Old Covenant could not equip the worshipper or complete him in that which he lacked in order to have access and communion with God. It did not touch the conscience and there was no remission of sin. Man could not draw near to God with these gifts and sacrifices. The New Testament is the reality. (Hebrews 9:11-15) In this passage the reality of the new covenant is set forth in contrast to the symbolic, presented in the previous verses. Christ is the substance of Leviticus shadows.

C. Jesus' sacrifice compared to animal sacrifices (9:11-15)

But Christ being come an high priest of good things to come, by a greater and more perfect tabernacle, not made with hands, that is to say, not of this building; Neither by the blood of goats and calves, but by his own blood he entered in once into the holy place, having obtained eternal redemption for us. For if the blood of bulls and of goats, and the ashes of an heifer sprinkling the unclean, sanctifieth to the purifying of the flesh: How much more shall the blood of Christ, who through the eternal Spirit offered himself without spot to God, purge your conscience from dead works to serve the living God? And for this cause he is the mediator of the New Testament that by means of death, for the redemption of the transgressions that were under the first testament, they which are called might receive the promise of eternal inheritance.

Our High Priest had the perfect sacrifice that could do what the Old Testament sacrifices could not do. He had His own blood and entered the Most Holy Place (heaven – verse 24) to obtain eternal redemption for us. This needed to be done only once, unlike the Old Testament sacrifices that had to be repeated again and again because they could not really removed sin. (7:27; 9:12, 26-28; 10:10)

This redemption is eternal in that, as each sin is forgiven, that forgiveness is eternal – the sin will never again be held against us as under the Old Testament. The consequences are also eternal in that the end is eternal life, if we remain faithful. 3:6,14;5:5; 6:1; 9:14, 24, 28; 11:26; John 1:4; 20:31; 6:69; Acts 9:22; LK 2:26; 9:20. Jesus, "Christ, Christ"; Christ Jesus", Messiah Lord; the Christ of God; the Lord`s Christ, very Christ. *"But Christ being come a high priest."* But is the pivot upon which this argument swings. It introduces the contrast. The Leviticus priesthood could not bring perfection but Christ did. *"But Christ being come," "but when Christ appeared."* Christ was the point of demarcation between prophecy and fulfillment, between the Old Covenant and the New Covenant. (Psalm 40:7; Deuteronomy 18:15-18; Matthew 2:2; 11:3) *"of good things to come," "of good things realized."* These good things realized include the better covenant, the removal of the conscience, unrestricted access to God; and personal communion with the Father. The purpose of his ministry was "to make reconciliation for the sins of the people.

1. *A greater and more prefect tabernacle (vs. 11)*

The preposition "by" is translated meaning *"to pass through" or "with"*.

"By a greater and more perfect tabernacle" the tabernacle in which Christ ministered is described as *"a greater and more perfect tabernacle."*

His tabernacle (His humanity) is superior to the tabernacle of the old covenant. Two contrasts are noted here: *"a greater tabernacle"* who is the Lord of glory, God incarnate and the God-man while *"A more tabernacle"* this phrase has respect to the sacred use of the tabernacle. The body of Christ was more perfectly fitted and suited as a tabernacle.

2. *Mediated by better blood (vs. 12)*
   "Not by the blood of goats and calves, but by his own blood." (Leviticus 16:14, 15)

3. *Wrought by a better method (vs. 12)*

By his own blood, he entered in once. He entered heaven as the surety and foremen for those whose hope is in him (6:20).

4. *Brings a better blessing (vs. 12)*

"Having obtained external redemption for us"
The word redemption means "to release on receipt of ransom" to redeem or liberate by payment of a ransom" Christ has purchased us by his own blood. This ransom price was paid to God who was offended (9:9, Matthew 20:28; 1 Tim 2:6) "Having obtained external redemption

for us." The word "obtained" means "to find" not "to acquire"

5. *Brings a better guarantee (VV. 13, 14)*

The Leviticus economy required two remedies:
a) The blood for atonement - Lev. 16; "the blood of goats and bulls") only provided temporary cleansing, but the sacrifice ("blood") of Jesus Christ provided permanent "cleansing." "The blood of goats and bulls" adequately removed ceremonial guilt, but it could not remove moral guilt.
b) The ashes for purification (Psalm 119:9; John 15:3; Eph 5:26 John 13:1-10) - The ashes of a heifer" removed ritual pollution, but they could not remove spiritual defilement.
The phrase "offered Himself" means that he did it voluntary because he delighted in doing the Father`s will. Jesus was "Without spot", he was spotless, stainless nature, sinless life, holy, harmless, undefiled, separated from sinners, just as the animals under Leviticus system were physically unblemished according to ceremonial standards. (7:26)

6. *Brings a better result (vs. 14)*

How much more shall the blood of Christ, who through the eternal Spirit offered himself without spot to God, purge your conscience from dead works to serve the living God? It seems that the writer has chosen this unusual way of referring to the Holy Spirit to bring out the truth that there is an eternal aspect to Christ's saving work."[10] (10:1-4; 6:1; 9:14; Titus 1:16; Colossians1:21) "Dead works" are those referring to the Mosaic Covenant (6:1), though some commentators take them as referring to works of the flesh that result in spiritual defilement.[11] They were "dead," in that they did not impart spiritual life other than only covering sin. According to P. E. Hughes, the word "dead" can be explained in three ways: (i) they proceed from him who is dead toward God, (ii) they are essentially sterile and unproductive (iii) they end in death.[12]" ... for the author of Hebrews [syneidesis] *conscience* is the internal faculty within man that causes him to be painfully aware of his sinfulness and, as a result, to experience a sense of guilt."[13]

7. Old Testament saints receive inheritance (vs. 15)

And for this cause he is the mediator of the New Testament which by means of death, for the redemption of the transgressions *that were* under the first testament, they which are called might receive the promise of

---

[10]Morris, p. 87.
[11]3E.g., Bruce, The Epistle ..., pp. 206-7.
[12]P. E. Hughes, A Commentary ..., pp. 360-61.
[13]Gary S. Selby, "The Meaning and Function of Syneidesis in Hebrews 9 and 10," Restoration Quarterly 28:3 (Third Quarter 1985/86):148.

eternal inheritance. (Rom 3:25; Acts 2:39; Gal 3:18; Heb 6:15-18, Titus 1:1; Rom 4:14; 16)Knowing that we have obtained "eternal redemption" (v. 12) through the death of Jesus our Mediator and the "eternal Holy Spirit"(vs.14), we can have hope in obtaining "eternal inheritance" but our forefathers under the Old Covenant enjoyed temporary blessings.

D. The Shedding of Blood (9:16-23)

The phrase *"For where a testament is,"* (vs.16) Even this one passage is a sufficient proof, that this letter was not written in Hebrew. The word "For" means in Hebrew a *covenant* not a *testament*; but in Greek, [διαθήκη], includes both ideas. He now gives its secondary meaning, holding that the promises should not have been ratified and valid, had they not been sealed by the death of Christ. Therefore, the new covenant is sealed with better blood. (9:16-22) *"Whereupon neither the first,"* (vs.18) Christ is the mediator of the new covenant in his blood (LK 22:20; 1 Cor 11:25). A mediator is an umpire, an arbitrator, one who intervenes between two parties either to make or restore peace to form a compact or ratify a covenant (Gal 3:20). A mediator is required only where two contracting parties, each party having a condition to fulfill in the contract. (Gen 15 and 17) Therefore, Moses also was a mediator between God and Israel. (Lev 26:46) The author then says that the Old Covenant was *dedicated with blood.* Even though the blood of beasts was shed, there was however, it did not release an everlasting covenant.

"For when Moses had spoken,"(vs.19) The author is explaining the custom of sprinkling which he quotes from Moses. He first teaches us that the covenant was consecrated, not that it had in itself anything wicked; but as there is nothing so holy that men by their filth will not defile, apart from God preventing it by making a renewal of all things. Therefore, the dedication was made on account of men, who alone wanted it.

"Moreover he sprinkled with blood,"(vs.21) He then adds, that the *tabernacle and all the vessels,* and also the very *book* of the law, were *sprinkled;* by which rite the people were then taught, that God could not be looked to for salvation, nor rightly worshipped, apart from having faith in an intervening blood. The animal blood dedicated diverse parts of the Old Covenant just like Jesus' blood dedicates us to God by forgiving our sins and affords to us a free access to God. These sacrifices purified the articles of the Old Covenant, but better sacrifices were needed for the better covenant. God required the *shedding of blood* (death) for forgiveness under the Mosaic Law. Thus all kinds of worship are then faulty and impure until Christ cleanses them by the sprinkling of his blood.

The author says the "copies of things in heaven" were purified by animal blood, but the "heavenly things themselves" with better sacrifices. (8:5) The *"heavenly things"* may refer to the consciences of men and women. It seems more likely, however, that they refer to the things connected with the heavenly tabernacle. While animal blood sufficiently cleansed the prototype on earth (copies of the things in heaven) under the Old Covenant, a "better" sacrifice was necessary to cleanse the realities in heaven. (cf. 8:5; 9:24) Clearly we need Jesus' sacrifice in order to go to heaven. Jesus Christ's death was essential for our salvation. But the contrast to the copies seems to imply that it was the whole gospel system and all its arrangements that were somehow purified by Jesus' sacrifice. (vs. 23) Possibly, the copies were "purified" (cleansed), but the heavenly things themselves were basically sanctified or set apart to God's service.

E. The better sacrifice offered only once (Hebrews 9:24-28)

The Old Testament sacrifices had to be repeated every year as the high priest would go into the Most Holy Place, but Jesus did not have to offer Himself repeatedly. That would require Him to suffer repeatedly from the foundation of the world. He was sacrificed once to put away sin. *"For Christ is not entered,"* (vs.24) He had spoken of the true sanctuary where Christ entered as heavenly. *The holy places* he takes for the sanctuary; he says that it is *not made with hands* because it is not made with the created things which are subject to decay. The author does not mean here the *heaven* we see in which the stars shine, but it is the glorious kingdom of God which is above all the heavens. He calls the old sanctuary the [ἀντίτυπον], the antitype of the true, that is, of the spiritual; for all the external figures represented as in a mirror what would have otherwise been above our corporeal senses. *"Now to appear,"* The Greek word (to appear) means to *manifest, display, to view, and to present one's self* in the sight of another. The phrase "Shall he appear the second time" explains that the word for *appear* means *"to be seen."* Like the appearance of Christ after His resurrection. The three appearing (VV 24, 26, 28) correspond to events which took place on the Day of Atonement. (Lev 26) We too "look for Him" – literally, "wait for him" (Phil 3:20; 1 Thessalonians 1:9, 10).

In the ninth chapter of the letter, the author has shown; that the earthly sanctuary was symbolic; (VV1-5) that the Leviticus priesthood was temporary; (VV 6-10) that the new covenant is the reality; (VV 11-15) that the new covenant is sealed with better blood. (VV 16-22)

"Nor yet that he should offer himself often," (vs.25) He explains that even under the Law there were days appointed for the chief sacrifices every year; they had also their hours daily morning and evening. The true sacrifice which Christ offered once for all is ever effective and his eternal priesthood should be sustained. He notices one difference as to the kind of sacrifice, for

Christ offered himself and not an animal; and he repeated not his sacrifice, as under the Law, for sacrifices were offered frequently and even persistently. *"For then must he often have suffered,"*(vs.26) *He* shows how it is senseless if we do not count it enough that expiation has been made by the one sacrifice of Christ and that the virtue of the one sacrifice is eternal and extends to all ages. And he says *since the foundation of the world,* or from the beginning of the world.

"And as it is appointed unto men," (vs.27) This double appointment mentioned here is a penal one. it is the sentence and course of a broken law, inflicting death upon Adam's race: (Rom 5:12) (i) *Death* is appointed to us to occur once. This is true for all of us, and has been ever since Adam's sin. (Genesis 3:19) Death is not a thing repeated daily or even frequently. For each individual, death is a one-time event. This, of course, refers to physical death which is the separation of the spirit from the body. (James 2:26) There is a spiritual death in which our sin separates us from God (Ephesians 2). There is also a second death in the lake of fire (Revelation 20:14). But this is not "appointed" for men in that, unlike physical death, we can avoid the second death. Further, that second death is spiritual, not physical. (ii) After death we face the *judgment*. Death is not the end of all. Judgment is sure to follow (Acts 17:31, Rom 2:5, 6, Rev 20:11-15). But since there will be a judgment after death, those whom He has saved

should eagerly await for His return when He will come a second time. This is when the judgment will occur (2 Corinthians 5:10; Matthew 25:31-46; Revelation 20; etc.)

Hebrews 10

F. The insufficiency of Animal Sacrifices (10:1-4)

The phrase *"For the Law having a shadow,"* He has borrowed this similitude from the pictorial art; for a shadow here is in a sense different from what it has in Colossians 2:17; where he calls the ancient rites or ceremonies shadows, because they did not possess the real substance of what they represented. "The 'shadow' Gr. [skia] then is the preliminary outline that an artist may make before he gets to his colors, and the [eikon] [lit. Image, "form"] is the finished portrait.This in distinct representation is called by the Greeks [σκιαγραφία], which you might call in Latin, [umbratilem], shadowy. The Greeks had also the [εἰκὼν], the full likeness, and so [eiconia] are called images (imagines) in Latin, which represent to the life the form of men or of animals or of places.This should have been clear simply by the fact God required them to keep offering the sacrifices every year. If a perfect sacrifice had been offered, then there would have been no more need to offer sacrifices. Once that sacrifice applied to any individual for his sins, his conscience would no longer be guilty "no more consciousness of sins", and there would be no need to offer sacrifice for the sins again. But as it was under the law, even if specific sacrifice had been offered for a sin, that sin would be remembered again every year and sacrifice would have to be offered for it again on the Day of Atonement. (Leviticus 16:11-15) *"Of good things to come,"* These are eternal things. The author's words mean that we have a lively image of future blessings. He then understands that spiritual pattern, the full fruition of which is delayed to the resurrection and the future world. *"Which they offered year by year,"* He speaks especially of the yearly sacrifice, mentioned in Leviticus 16, though all the sacrifices are here included under one kind. Now he reasons thus: When there is no longer any consciousness of sin, there is then no need of sacrifice; but under the Law the offering of the same sacrifice was often repeated; then no satisfaction was given to God, nor was guilt removed nor were consciences appeased; were it otherwise there would have been made an end of sacrificing. (vs.2) The old Sacrifices were a failure in three ways: They could not bring access to God, they could not remove sin and they were only external. It was "impossible for the blood of bulls and goats to take away sins because of God's eternal purpose. God planned to have a perfect human sacrifice not just animal sacrifice.

"A remembrance again,"(vs.3) Though the Gospel is a message of reconciliation with God, yet it is necessary

that we should daily remember our sins; but what the author means is that sins were brought to remembrance that guilt might be removed by the means of the sacrifice then offered. It is not, then, any kind of remembrance that is here meant, but that which might lead to such a confession of guilt before God, as rendered a sacrifice necessary for its removal.

But since the author concludes that the sacrifices of the Law were weak, because they were every year repeated in order to obtain pardon, for the very same reason it may be concluded that the sacrifice of Christ was weak, if it must be daily offered, in order that its virtue may be applied to us.

"For it is not possible,"(vs.4) He confirms the former sentiment with the same reason which he had adduced before, that the blood of beasts could not cleanse souls from sin. The Jews, indeed, had in this a symbol and a pledge of the real cleansing; but it was with reference to another, even as the blood of the calf represented the blood of Christ. *"Take away"* (vs.4) is the Greek word [aphaireo] which is used of a literal taking off. The good example is that of Peter when he cutting off the ear of the high priest's slave (Luke 22:50), or figuratively as of the removal of reproach. (Luke 1:25)

G. God's eternal will (10:5-10)

The author then quotes an Old Testament passage from Psalms 40:6ff showing that God was not satisfied with

Old Testament sacrifices. So the Christ would have to come to do God's will as it had been spoken of in God's book. David originally stated this; but here, as he often did, he spoke in the first person though really giving a prophecy of the Christ. (Acts 2) The sacrifices made by the people in the Old Testament did not really satisfy the demands of God's justice. Therefore, someone had to come who could accomplish God's will in this matter. *"Wherefore, when he cometh,"*(vs.5) this entering into the world was the manifestation of Christ in the flesh; for when he put on man's nature that he might be a Redeemer to the world and appeared to men, he is said to have then come into the world, as elsewhere he is said to have descended from heaven.

"But a body hast thou prepared me," the words of David are different, "An ear hast thou bored for me," a phrase which some think has been borrowed from an ancient rite or custom of the Law, (Exodus 21:6) for if any one set no value on the liberty granted at the jubilee, and wished to be under perpetual servitude, his ear was bored with an awl. The meaning, as they think was this, "Thou shalt have me, O Lord, as a servant forever." Psalm 40:6 reads: "My ears Thou hast opened (or dug, [i.e., cleaned out])," whereas Hebrews 10:5 says: "a body Thou hast prepared for me." The idea is the same, the former expression being a figurative citation (Exod. 21:6; cf. Isa. 50:4-5), and the latter a literal description. God had prepared His servant to hear His Word so that he would

obey it.However, take another view, regarding it as intimating obedience for we are deaf until God opens our ears, that is, until he corrects the stubbornness that cleaves us.

God took away the first (old sacrifice) to make way for the second. God's focus was always the second covenant, the superior one. That second covenant has now come in Jesus Christ.In any case; it is clear that Psalm 40:6-8 is saying that the sacrifices and burnt offerings were inadequate. So here is at least the fourth Old Testament proof that there must be a change of the law. The "roll (scroll) of the book" is the written instruction (torah) of God. In the Old Testament, the prophets presented Messiah as committed to doing God's will entirely. (1) Hebrews 7:11-14 showed that the law had to change because the priesthood was inadequate, and Psalm 110 predicted a priest of a different order. (2) Hebrews 8:6-13 quoted Jeremiah 31:31ff which directly said the Old Testament would be replaced by a New Testament. (3) Hebrews 6:13-20 – God had made a promise to Abraham of a blessing on all nations. That promise was not fulfilled under the Old Testament but is fulfilled in Christ under the gospel. And now (4) quotes Psalm 40:6-8, showing that the sacrifices of the Old Testament were inadequate, so another sacrifice would come.Jesus' sacrifice is effective as it sanctifies the believer making him holy. (10:5-7) The old sacrifice had no way of making a man holy. One act provided permanent sanctification for everyone who trusts and believes in Jesus Christ. (Col. 2:10)

H. Jesus the Perfect Sacrifice (10:11-18)

The phrase *"And every priest,"* (vs.11) here is the conclusion of the whole argument, — that the practice of daily sacrificing is inconsistent with and wholly foreign to the priesthood of Christ; and that hence after his coming the Levitical priests whose custom and settled practice was daily to offer, were deposed from their office; for the character of things which are contrary is, that when one thing is set up, the other falls to the ground. The author is defending the priesthood of Christ; the conclusion then is that the ancient priesthood, which is inconsistent with this, has ceased; for all the saints find a full consecration in the one offering of Christ. At the same time the word [τετελείωκεν], which is rendered "has consecrated," may hitherto be rendered "has perfected" We are told that the Old Testament priests repeatedly offered the same sacrifices, but those could not remove sin (verses 1-4). The Levitical priests never sat down for they stood *"daily"* because they never finished their work, but Jesus Christ "sat down" beside His Father, because He finished His work. But Jesus offered a sacrifice that did not need to be repeated "one" and "forever."(10:10) Jesus' sacrifice removes sin, which the old sacrifice could not remove.

"From henceforth expecting till his enemies," (vs.13) He is now waits until all his enemies be made a footstool (Phil 2:10). Christ's sacrifice gives believers eternal perfection which is eternal salvation and the forgiveness of sins as permanent in the new sacrifice. In the new covenant God said, "He would put his laws upon their heart and upon their mind; he will no more remember their sins." The new sacrifice was efficient for the reason that it had fulfilled his promises.

When it says sins are remembered no more, does that mean the event is completely gone from God's memory, so He does not even know it happened. This cannot be. God knows everything. If it happened as historical fact, then God remembers it in the sense that He is aware it happened. To say He forgives our sins "remembers them no more" does not in any way mean the sin is no longer in God's ability to recall. The proof of this is the fact that many sins, for which men repented and were forgiven, are yet recorded in the Scriptures. Consider Peter's denial of Christ, Paul's persecution of Christians, as well as numerous other Old and New Testament sins. These were clearly forgiven by God and so, "remembered no more." Yet here is the record of them in Scripture! How can it be said God is not even aware of them, when we see them recorded in His word?

By saying, *"them who are sanctified,"* (vs.13) he includes all the children of God; and he reminds us that the grace of sanctification is sought elsewhere in vain. But lest men should imagine that Christ is now idle in heaven, he repeats again that he *sat down at God's right hand;* by which phrase is denoted, as we have seen elsewhere, his dominion and power.Then Jesus sat down at the right hand of God. The fact that Jesus sat down after He offered His sacrifice is in contrast to the priests under the Old Law, whom the passage says stood ministering their sacrifices. They had to stand because they had to continue offering sacrifices. Jesus sat down because His work was done. He offered the complete, perfect sacrifice. No more sacrifice was needed.

At God's right hand is where, as we have repeatedly seen, it was prophesied He would sit when He reigned as Priest and King (1:3; 8:1; Psalms 110:1-4; etc.). He is therefore now Priest at God's right hand, and therefore He is now King. At God's right hand, the prophecy stated, His enemies would be made His footstool – i.e., they would all be subjugated before Him (Psalms 110:1-4; Hebrews 1:13). This ties to 1 Corinthians 15:20-28 which shows Jesus will **reign** till the last enemy has been put under His feet, and that will happen when death is destroyed by all being raised from the dead.

"Whereof the Holy Ghost also is a witness," (vs.15) the "Holy Spirit" testified through Jeremiah (Jer. 31:33-34; cf. Heb. 8:8-12), and continues to testify to us.

To say *"sins are remembered no more,"* (vs.17) means simply that the sins are not held against us. Since God is omniscient, He remembers everything, but He does not hold the forgiven sinner's sins against him or her. He will not recall the sin in a year or in a thousand years to hold us accountable and deserving to be punished. In contrast to animal sacrifices, Jesus' sacrifice remits sin so that we will never again be treated as though we stand guilty for that sin before God. (Genesis 41:51)

"Now where remission of these is," (vs.18) The author said, that final *"forgiveness"* at the Cross meant the end of sacrifices ("no longer any offering") for sin."The author is telling his hearers that it would be foolish to abandon Christianity to return to Judaism because Jesus' priesthood has brought the believers into full acceptance with God, which the Old Covenant could not.

IV. Applications to Faithfulness (10:19-13:25)

A. Drawing Near to God (10:19-39)

1. Holding Fast and Assembling with the Saints (10:19-25)

"Having therefore, brethren,"(vs,19) The author states the sum of his preceding doctrine, to which he then fitly subjoins a solemn exhortation, and denounces a ruthless

threatening on those who had renounced the grace of Christ. The allegory describes the access which Christ has opened to us; for he compares heaven to the old sanctuary and sets forth the things which have been spiritually accomplished in Christ in typical expressions. He says first that we have boldness to enter into the holiest. The Greek word [parresia], which appears in verse 19 *"boldness"* and in verse 35 *"boldness,"* forms an inclusion tying the thought together. This privilege was never granted to the fathers under the Law, for the people were forbidden to enter the visible sanctuary, though the high priest bore the names of the tribes on his shoulders, and twelve stones as a memorial of them on his breast. But now the case is very different, for not only symbolically, but in reality, an entrance into heaven is made open to us through the favor of Christ, for he has made us a royal priesthood. [14]

He further says, *by the blood of Jesus,* because the door of the sanctuary was not opened for the review entrance of the high priest, except through the intervention of blood. But he afterwards marks the difference between this blood and that of beasts; for the blood of beasts, as it

14 Macknight makes this "entrance" to be death! As though the Apostle was speaking of what was future, while in verse 22, with which the contents of this verse and the following are connected, he says, "let us draw near;" that is, we who have this entrance, even "the new and living way." Possessing such a privilege, they were to draw nigh. It is clearly an entrance and a way which believers now possess.

soon turns to corruption, could not long retain its usefulness; but the blood of Christ, which is subject to no corruption. His blood flows forever as a pure stream and is sufficient for us even to the end of the world. The beasts slain in sacrifice had no power to quicken, as they were dead; but Christ who arose from the dead to bestow life on us, communicates his own life to us.

"Through the veil," (vs.20) The veil covered the recesses of the sanctuary and afforded entrance there, so the divinity, though hid in the flesh of Christ leads us even into heaven because he is the door and the way. All believers now have an open invitation to come into "the holy place.Christ's glory in his body conceals as a veil the majesty of God, while it is also that which conducts us to the enjoyment of all the good things of God.We can now enter God's presence through Jesus' crucified flesh. Therefore, we can enter the Holiest place through the torn temple "veil." (Matt. 27:51) We have access to the throne of Grace through the finished work of Christ.

"And having a high priest,"(vs.20) The author has earlier said of the abrogation of the ancient priesthood, it behoves us now to bear in mind, for Christ could not be a priest without having the former priests divested of their office since it was another order.

"Let us draw near with a true heart," The Jews formerly cleansed themselves by various washings to prepare themselves for the service of God. It is no wonder that

the rites for cleansing were carnal, since the worship of God itself, involved in shadows, as yet partook in a manner of what was carnal. The word *true* here means Sincere and reliable. We should approach God with the "assurance" that Jesus Christ's death has removed our guilt for sin, and has made us acceptable to God. (9:13-14; Num. 8:7; Rom. 5:1; 8:1; cf. 1 John 1:9) For the priest, being a mortal, was chosen from among sinners to perform for a time sacred things; he was, indeed, adorned with precious vestments, but yet they were those of this world, that he might stand in the presence of God; he only came near the work of the covenant; and to sanctify his entrance, he borrowed for a sacrifice a brute animal either from herd or the flock. But Christ is not only pure and innocent but is also the fountain of all holiness and righteousness, and was constituted a priest by a heavenly oracle, not for the short period of a mortal life, but perpetually. Therefore, we have come to learn what must be the structure of our minds in order that we may enjoy the benefits conferred by Christ because there is no coming to him without an upright or a true heart, and a sure faith, and a pure conscience. Now, a true or sincere heart is opposed to a heart that is hypocritical and deceitful. [15]By the term full assurance, [πληροφορία] the

---

15This true, sincere, or upright heart, freed from vice and pollution, was symbolized by the washing at the end of the verse. Without washing the priests were not allowed to minister, and were

author points out the nature of faith, and at the same time reminds us, that the grace of Christ cannot be received except by those who possess a fixed and unwavering conviction. The sprinkling of the heart from an evil conscience takes place, either when we are, by obtaining pardon, deemed pure before God, or when the heart, cleansed from all corrupt affections, is not stimulated by the goads of the flesh. I am disposed to include both these things. [16]*Our bodies washed with pure water* is generally understood of baptism; but it seems most likely that the author alludes to the ancient ceremonies of the Law; and so by water he designates the Spirit of God,

---

threatened with death, Exodus 30:19-21; and when any of them touched an unclean thing, he was not allowed to eat of holy things until he washed himself, see 12:6 [sic]. Washing the body was a most important thing, as it symbolized the inward washing of the heart, which alone makes us true, or sincere, or faithful to God. We have here two things — a sincere heart, and assurance of faith: the last is then set forth by sprinkling, a word borrowed for Levitical rites; and the first by the washing of the body as under the law.

16 Πονηρὸς means in Hebrew, the evil of sin wicked, and also the effect of sin, miserable It seems to be in the latter sense here; a miserable conscience is one oppressed with guilt. So Grotius and Stuart regard the meaning. It is the same as "consciousness of sin" in verse 2. What seems to be meant is an accusing or guilty conscience, laboring under the pressure of conscious sin. But Doddridge and Scott, like Calvin, combine the two ideas of guilt and pollution; though washing, afterwards mentioned, appears more appropriately to refer to the latter; and forgiveness is what is most commonly connected with the blood of Christ.

according to what is said by Prophet Ezekiel, "I will sprinkle clean water upon you." (Ezekiel 36:25)

This means that we are made partakers of Christ, if we come to him, consecrated in body and soul; and that this consecration is not the procession of ceremonies but that which proceeds from faith in Jesus Christ. Thus, Paul exhorts the faithful to cleanse themselves from all filthiness of flesh and spirit, since they had been adopted by God as his children. (2 Corinthians 7:1)

"Let us hold fast," (vs.23) The author is exhorting the Jews to persevere and he mentions hope not faith because hope is produced from faith. We should not only exercise faith (v. 22), but also hope (v.23) and love. (v. 24) The second admonition, to *hold fast* to the confession of our hope, is what the author has emphasized most strongly in this letter.He requires also profession or confession, for it is not true faith except it shows itself before men. He therefore bids them not only to believe with the heart, but also to show and to profess how much they honored Christ.

"And let us consider one another," (v. 24) The other admonition addresses our responsibility to fellow believers. This admonition "to love" one another is our Christian obligation and necessary, since some were abandoning the faith. These Hebrew Christians needed *"to encourage one another"* to remain faithful to the

Lord, since we have a great High Priest who can help us (v. 21).

"Not forsaking the assembling of ourselves together," (v. 25) "Whatever the motivation, the writer regarded the desertion of the communal meetings as utterly serious. It threatened the corporate life of the congregation and almost certainly was a prelude to apostasy on the part of those who were separating themselves from the assembly ..."[17]Such apathy for one's fellow believers and forsaking the assembling of ourselves together shows unconcern for Christ himself and portends the danger of apostasy, concerning which our author is about to issue another earnest warning. (vv.26ff)[18]

2. Willful Sinning (10:26-31)

"For if we sin willfully," (vs.26) Willful Sinning means(1) Sin; (2) committed by someone who has a knowledge of the truth; (3) yet he sins willfully – this surely seems to imply that he knows he is doing something wrong, or at least that he has had plenty of opportunity to know; (4) he trods Jesus underfoot; (5) he has counted the blood of the covenant a common thing; (6) he has insulted the Spirit of grace; (7) there is no sacrifice for the sin but only judgment. *If we sin willfully, after that we have received the knowledge of the truth;* as

---

[17]Lane, Hebrews 9—13, p. 290. Cf. Robertson, 5:412.
[18]P. E. Hughes, A Commentary ..., p. 415.

though he had said, "If we knowingly and willingly renounce the grace which we had obtained." The word 'we' cannot refer to any other group of people than his readers and himself (2:1) And that the author here refers only to apostates is clear from the whole passage; for what he treats of is this, which those who had been once received into the Church ought not to forsake it, as some were wont to do. Therefore, if an apostate rejects Jesus Christ's sacrifice, there is nothing else that can protect him or her from God's judgment (cf. 6:6; Num. 15:30-31).He now declares that there remained for such no sacrifice for sin, because they had willfully sinned after having received the knowledge of the truth. He denies, then, that any sacrifice remains for them who renounce the death of Christ, which is not done by any offense except by a total renunciation of the faith. But as to sinners who fall in any other way (backslide), Christ offers himself daily to them, so that they are to seek no other sacrifice for expiating their sins.

"Who has trodden underfoot the Son of God,"(vv. 27,28,29) There is this likeness between apostates under the Law and under the Gospel, that both perish without mercy; but the kind of death is different; for the author denounces on the despisers of Christ not only the deaths of the body, but eternal perdition. And therefore he says that a sorer punishment awaits them. And he designates the desertion of Christianity by three things; for he says that thus the Son of God is trodden under foot that his

blood is counted an unholy thing, and that despite is done to the Spirit of grace. Now, it is a more heinous thing to tread under foot than to despise or reject; and the dignity of Christ is far different from that of Moses; and further, he does not simply set the Gospel in opposition to the Law, but the person of Christ and of the Holy Spirit to the person of Moses. *"The blood of the covenant,"* The author enhances ingratitude by a comparison with the benefits. It is the greatest indignity to count the blood of Christ unholy, by which our holiness is affected; this is done by those who depart from the faith. Since an Israelite who rejects the Old Covenant suffered a severe penalty, we in the Age of Grace will suffer an even greater penalty if we reject the better New Covenant. Apostasy under the New Covenant has great consequence when you trample under foot "the Son of God" by despising Him by having publicly rejected His salvation. This as well involves despising the better "blood" of Jesus Christ that "sanctified" the apostate (who is a Christian; cf. vv. 10, 14). Besides, the apostate has insulted the Holy Spirit; the Spirit of grace who graciously brought him or her to faith in Christ.

He calls it the blood of the covenant, because then only was the promises made sure to us when this pledge was added. But he points out the manner of this confirmation by saying that we are sanctified; for the bloodshed would avail us nothing, except we were sprinkled with it by the Holy Spirit; and hence come our expiation and sanctification. He then alludes to the ancient rite of sprinkling, which availed not to real sanctification, but was only its shadow or image. *"The Spirit of grace,* "The author says the Spirit of grace from the effects produced; for it is by the Spirit and through his influence that we receive the grace offered to us in Christ. For the spirit enlightens our minds by faith, seals the adoption of God on our hearts, which regenerates us unto newness of life, who grafts us into the body of Christ, which he may live in us and we in him. He is therefore rightly called the Spirit of grace and by whom Christ becomes ours with all his blessings. But to despise him, or to treat him with scorn, by which we are endowed with so many benefits, is a transgression and wicked. All who willfully render useless his grace, by which they had been favored, act scornfully towards the Spirit of God. It is therefore no wonder that God so severely visits blasphemies of this kind; it is no wonder that he shows himself inevitable towards those who tread under foot Christ the Mediator, who alone reconciles us to himself; it is no wonder that he closes up the way of salvation against those who spurn the Holy Spirit, the only true guide.

"Vengeance belongeth unto me,"(vs.30) Though then the design of Moses was to console the faithful, as they would have God as the avenger of wrongs done to them; yet we may always conclude from his words that it is the peculiar office of God to take vengeance on the ungodly. Nor does he pervert his testimony that hence proves that

the contempt of God will not be unpunished; for he is a righteous judge who claims to himself the office of taking vengeance.

"It is a fearful thing to fall into the hands of God," (vs.31) Moses warned the Israelites against apostatizing. That was what the author was talking about and explains it as a "terrifying" prospect for a believer who has renounced his or her faith, "to fall" under God's hand of chastisement.

3. The past sacrifices and sufferings (10:32-39)

The author concluded his warning, by reminding his readers of their former faithfulness when they were being tempted, in order to encourage them to endure their present and future tests. (cf. 4:12-16; 6:9-20) The combination of 10:26-31 and 32-35 suggests that it may have been the experience of suffering, abuse, and loss in the world that caused these Hebrew Christians reject Christ and the assembling together as mentioned in v 25. Some of his hearers had proved faithful in severe trials of their faith and finally they endured and stood their ground and when others had encouraged them to abandon it, and they had withstood public shame and persecution (reproaches and tribulations) for their faith. They had also unashamedly supported other believers who had under gone persecution in the same way. (Became sharers with those who were so treated)

"In the world of the first century the lot of prisoners was difficult. Prisoners were to be punished, not pampered. Little provision was made for them, and they were dependent on friends for their supplies [including food]. For Christians visiting prisoners was a meritorious act. (Matt 25:36) But there was some risk, for the visitors became identified with the visited. The readers of the epistle had not shrunk from this. It is not pleasant to endure ignominy and it is not pleasant to be lumped with the ignominious. They had endured both."They had also been willing to suffer material loss ("accepted... the seizure of your property"), because they looked forward to a "better inheritance (possession)" in the future. (cf. Luke21:19) Moreover, they had done this "joyfully," not grudgingly."The eternal inheritance laid up for them was so real in their eyes that they could light heartedly bid farewell to material possessions which were short lived in any case. This attitude of mind is precisely that 'faith' of which our author goes on to speak."

"It is a truth of life that in many ways it is easier to stand adversity than it is to stand prosperity. Ease has ruined far more men than trouble ever did."(10:35-36) Now was not the time to discard ("do not throw away") that "confidence" in a better reward. (cf. 3:6; 4:16; 10:19) They needed "endurance" to persevere, to "keep on keeping on," as the saying goes. By doing this, they would do God's "will," and eventually "receive what [He] promised," namely, an eternal reward. (1:14; 3:14;

9:15; Matt. 6:19) This exhortation is a good summary of the whole message of Hebrews. What they had endured for Christ's sake entitled them to a reward. Let them not throw it away. The NT does not reject the notion that Christians will receive rewards, though, of course, that is never the prime motive for service.

The safeguard against degeneration, isolation, and consequent failure is to make progress in the Christian life, and to proceed from point to point from an elementary to the richest, fullest, deepest experience. If the writer's concern had been the salvation of those readers who were unbelievers, this would have been an opportune time for him to exhort them to believe in Christ. He could have written, For you have need of regeneration. Instead, he exhorted his readers to endure rather than apostatize.

"Perseverance is one of the great unromantic virtues. Most people can start well; almost everyone can be fine in spasms. Most people have their good days. Most men have their great moments. To everyone it is sometimes given to mount up with wings as eagles; in the moment of the great effort everyone can run and not be weary; but the greatest gift of all is to walk and not to faint."10:37-38 After all, we will not have long to persevere. The Lord's return is near, "in a very little while." (Rev. 22:20)

In the mean time, we need to keep walking "by faith." If we abandon that purpose *"shrink back"*, we will not please God. This observation (vs. 38b) is a figure of speech called litotes in which a positive idea is expressed by negating the opposite. As the larger context makes plain, he means, 'God will be severely angered.' (vs. 27) The allusions made in these verses are to Isaiah 26:21 and Habakkuk 2:3-4 in the Septuagint. The author took all of his Old Testament quotations from this version, except the one in10:30, which he took from the Hebrew Bible. "My righteous one" refers to an individual believer. "Shrinking back" refers to apostasy."Paul is concerned with the way a man comes to be accepted by God; the author of this letter is concerned with the importance of holding fast to one's faith in the face of temptations to abandon it."The author assumed hopefully that his Christian readers, along with himself, would not apostatize. Destruction or ruin could refer either to eternal damnation in hell or to temporal punishment. In view of what has preceded in the epistle, the latter alternative is probably in view (cf. Matt. 26:8; Mark 14:4; Acts 25:16). The writer did not want his readers to be the objects of God's discipline.

Probably *waste* is the best translation for this word *destruction* in Hebrews 10:39. A believer who does not walk by faith goes back into the old ways and wastes his life. Likewise, the positive alternative set forth at the end of this verse is not a reference to conversion. It refers to the preservation of the faithful believer's full sanctification until he receives his full reward (cf. 1 Pet. 2:9). The *preserving of the soul* is equivalent to *saving the life* (cf. James 5:20)."This meaning agrees well with the exposition of 10:32-39. The readers were to live by faith in the midst of difficult times. The result of obedience to the Word of God would be a life-preserving walk instead of temporal discipline, the loss of physical life."This is the most direct and severe of all the warnings in Hebrews. In view of the Son's priestly ministry (5:1—10:18), apostasy is a sin that will draw terrible consequences for the believer. It will not result in the loss of eternal salvation, but the loss of some, or possibly a major portion of, one's eternal reward.

The nature of the writer's response to the men and women he addressed confirms the specifically pastoral character of the parenesis, in which he closely identifies himself with his audience. The severity with which he writes of apostasy and of the destructive lifestyle of those who have deserted the house church expresses anguish and compassionate concern that Christians should not be subverted by a form of worldliness that would separate them from the life and truth they have received from Christ and from one another.

Hebrews 11

B. Old Covenant Examples of Faithfulness (chapter 11)

1. Faith as defined by Hebrew (11:1-3)

"Now faith is the substance of things hoped for, the evidence of things not seen." (vs. 1) The opening *"Now"* has almost the force of *"for,"* denoting a further confirmation of what had just been declared. At the close of chapter 10 the apostle had just affirmed that the saving of the soul is obtained through believing, where upon he now takes occasion to show what faith is and does. It is important to bear in mind at the outset that Hebrews 11 is an amplification and exemplification of Hebrews 10:38, 39: the "faith" which the author is describing and illustrating is that which has the saving of the soul. The Verses 6-8-thing described is Faith; the description is this: 'It is the substance of things hoped for' etc. The acts of faith are two: it is the substance, it is the evidence. Think it not strange that I call them *acts,* for that. There is a great deal of difference between the

acts of faith and the effects of faith. The contents of verse 1 do not furnish so much a formal definition of faith, as they supply a terse description of how it operates and what it produces. First, He tells us that "faith is the substance of things hoped for." The Greek word rendered "substance" has been variously translated. The margin of the A.V. gives "ground or confidence." The R.V. has "assurance" in the text, and "giving substance to" in the margin. The Greek word is [hypostasis] and is rendered "confident."

From what has just been said, the reader will perhaps perceive better the force of the rather peculiar word "substance" in the text of the A.V. It comes from two Latin words, *sub stans* meaning "standing under." "Faith is the *substance* of things hoped for": as the marginal reading of the R.V. suggests, "giving substance to." It is resting upon His promises, and expecting the accomplishment of them, faith gives the object hoped for at a *future* period, a *present* reality and power in the soul, as if already possessed; for the believer is satisfied with the security afforded, and *acts* under the full persuasion that God will not fail of His engagement. Faith provides a firm standing-ground while I await the fulfilment of God's promises. Faith gives the soul an *appropriating hold* of them. "Faith is a firm persuasion and expectation that God will perform all that He has promised to us in Christ; and this persuasion is so strong that it gives the soul a kind of possession and present fruition of those things, gives them a subsistence in the soul by the first fruits and foretastes of them; so that believers in the exercise of faith are filled with joy unspeakable and full of glory." (Matthew Henry) Faith is a grace which unites subject and object: there is no need to ascend to Heaven, for faith makes distant things nigh. (Romans 10:6, 7) Faith, then, is the bond of union between the soul and the things God has promised. By believing we "receive"; by believing in Christ, He becomes *ours* (John 1:12)

Faith is the *confidence* of things hoped for." It is a firm persuasion of that which is hoped for, because it assures its possessor not only that there *are* such things, but that through the power and faithfulness of God he shall yet possess them. Faith and confidence are inseparable: just so far as I am counting upon the ability and reliability of the Promiser, shall I be confident of receiving the things promised and which I am expecting. "We *believe* and are *sure."* (John 6:69)

Faith is evident by its fruits, works, and effects. Faith is *"the evidence of things not seen."* The Greek noun here rendered "evidence" ("proving" in the R.V., with "test" in the margin) is derived from a verb which signifies to *convince,* and that by demonstration. It was used by the Lord Jesus when He uttered that challenge, "which of you convicteth me of sin?" (John 8:46) The noun occurs in only one other place, namely, 2 Timothy 3:16, "All scripture is... profitable for doctrine, for *reproof,"* or "conviction"—to give assurance and certainty of what is true. Therefore, the word "evidence" in our text denotes teat which furnishes proof, so that one is assured of the reality and certainty of things Divine. "Faith," then, is first the *hand* of the soul which "lays hold of" the contents of God's promises; second, it is the *eye* of the soul which looks out toward and represents them clearly and convincingly to us. The conviction is so powerful that the heart is influenced thereby, and the will moved to conform thereto. Most of the examples given in chapter 11 involve a person acting confidently in accordance with what God says. By Faith Abel offered to God a better sacrifice, Noah built an ark, Abraham obeyed by leaving his nation and so the list continues. The author uses words of action in verses 32-34: they conquered, administered, gained, quenched etc. Faith acts out of a bold confidence.

"For by it the elders obtained a good report,"(vs.2) Having described the principal qualities of faith, the apostle now proceeds to give further proof of its Excellency, as is evident from the opening "For." It is by faith we are approved of God. By the "elders" is signified those who lived informer times, namely, the Old Covenant saints—included among the "fathers" or Hebrews 1:1. It was not by their sociability, genuineness, seriousness, or any other natural high calibre, but by *faith* that the ancients *"obtained a good report."* This affirmation was made by the author with the purpose of

reminding the Hebrews that their pious progenitors were justified by faith, and to the end of the chapter he shows that *faith* was the standard of all their holy obedience, eminent services, and patient sufferings in the cause of God. The Greek for *"obtained a good report"* is not in the active voice, but the passive: literally, "were witnessed of," an honourable testimony being borne to them—cf., verses 4, 5. God took care that a record should be kept (complete in Heaven, in part transcribed in the Scriptures) of all the works of their faith. God has borne witness to the fact that Enoch "walked with Him" (Gen. 5:24), that David was "a man after His own heart" (1 Sam. 13:14), that Abraham was His "friend." (2 Chron. 20:7) This testimony of His acceptance of them because of their faith was borne by God. God gave them His Spirit who assured them of their acceptance: Psalm 51:12, Acts 15:8. Let us therefore, learn to esteem what God does; let us value a Christian not for his intellect, natural charms, or social position, but for his *faith,* evidenced by an obedient walk and godly life.

"Through faith we understand that the worlds were framed,"(Vs. 3) This extends not only to how the universe ("worlds") came into being (cf. 1:2-3), but how it will end as well."There are two views explaining the origin of this universe. One is speculation, and the other is revelation. The origin of the universe presents a problem which neither science nor philosophy can solve

as is obvious from their conflicting attempts; but that complexity vanishes exclusively before faith.

The first view regarding the author's choice of Gk [aion] age, rather than cosmos world, is that he referred to ages in expectation of the list of the heroes, who lived in various ages. If this view is correct, then verse 3 is more of a commentary on God's creation of history than it is on His creation of the cosmos. The last part of verse 3 may seem to contradict this view, but *"what is seen"* could refer to what is seen in history, rather than what is seen in the material world.

The second view is that Gk [aion] is basically a synonym for cosmos here and refers to the universe of time and space. This word [Aion] seems to be used this way in 1:2, as well. Possibly the author chose [aion] here to emphasize the temporal progression of God's creation, rather than its physicality. Many of the commentators favour this view for they believe that the author was looking back on the creation account in Genesis, rather than forward to what he would say in the rest of chapter 11. "Belief in the existence of the world is not faith, nor is it faith when men hold that the world was made out of some pre-existing 'stuff.' The author did not say that God created the universe out of nothing (creation ex nihilo), an idea that the Greeks rejected but said that the universe did not originate from original material or anything observable. Genesis 1:1-3 and logic seem to indicate that

God did indeed create the universe, something visible
("what is seen"), out of His word, something invisible
[τὰἀο ρατα] ("not visible")."Had the visible world been
formed out of materials which were subject to human
observation, there would have been no room for faith.

But there is no authority for making [ἐκ] and[
φαινομένων] one word as he proposes: yet if the
transposition of [μὴ] be admitted, which both ancient
and modern critics allow, the meaning advocated by
Calvin may still be defended: "in order that of things not
apparent there might be things visible;" the things not
apparent or visible being the power, wisdom and
goodness of God, in exact harmony with Romans 1:20,
where God's power and divinity are said to be "invisible
things" [τὰἀο ρατα]: they are things not apparent. Again,
the verb [κατηρτίσθαι] denotes not creation, but the
fitting or adjusting, or setting in order of things.

If, then, the words were rendered literally, the meaning
would be as follows, *"So that they became the visible of
things not visible,"* or, not apparent. Thus the preposition
would be joined to the participle to which it belongs.
Besides, the words would then contain a very important
truth, that we have in this visible world, a noticeable
image of God; and thus the same truth is taught here, as
in Romans 1:20, where it is said, that the invisible things
of God are made known to us by the creation of the
world, they being seen in his works. God has given us,
throughout the whole framework of this world, clear

evidences of his eternal wisdom, goodness, and power; and though he is in himself invisible. God in a manner becomes visible to us in his works. Correctly then is this world called the mirror of divinity; not that there is sufficient clearness for man to gain a full knowledge of God, by looking at the world, but that he has thus so far revealed himself, that the ignorance of the ungodly is without excuse. The faithful to whom he has given eyes, see sparks of his glory, as it were, glittering in every created thing. Thus the world was no doubt made, that it might be the theater of the divine glory. It hence appears that the reference here is to the setting in order of this world, and not to the first creation of its materials; and if so, the second clause cannot refer to the creation of the world out of nothing, as it is necessarily connected with what the first clause contains. "Faith" then refers here, if this view must be taken, not to the fact that the world was made by God, which even heathens admitted, but to the design of God in creation, the manifestation of his own glory. "The heavens," says the Psalmist "declare the glory of God."

2. The more excellent Sacrifice (11:4)

"By faith Abel offered unto God a more excellent sacrifice," (vs. 4) The author's object in this chapter is to show, that however excellent were the works of the saints, it was from faith they derived their value, their worthiness, and all their excellences; and hence follows

what he has already intimated, that the fathers pleased God by faith alone. The readers could identify with "Abel" because he, too, had an "excellent sacrifice." Those who based their hope of God's acceptance on an inferior sacrifice, as in Judaism, would experience disappointments, as "Cain" did. The faith of Abel laid hold of Christ as truly as does ours. God has had but one way of salvation since sin entered the world: "by grace, through faith, not of works." They are disgustingly mistaken who suppose that under the old covenant people were saved by keeping the law. The "fathers" had the same promises we have, not merely of Canaan, but of heaven. (Hebrews 11:16) Wherever the word faith is found in this chapter, we must bear in mind, which the author speaks of it so that the Jews might regard no other rule than God's word, and might also depend alone on his promises. Abel's offering was more acceptable than that of Cain, because he had faith." — Grotius. By the way, what made Abel's offering more acceptable that that of Cain was markedly its being an offering of the "firstlings" (firstborn), and its inclusion of the "fat" (4:4). Abel's offering, according to the account given, was not in the number or quantity, but in quality. Ancient near Easterners commonly held that a deity deserved the first of the "fat," which represented the best part of an animal offering. Along the same line, by offering a blood sacrifice, Abel offered the most precious thing that life supplies. The word "sacrifice," θυσία, means properly an offered victim, but sometimes anything offered to God. Certainly, Abel's sacrifice is called in Genesis 4:4, an offering. The word πλείων is literally more, but is used in the sense of more in number, quantity or excellency. Scripture indicates that the superior quality of Abel's offering was derived from the integrity of his heart rather than from the nature of the offering itself. (Gen 4:7) Therefore, what gave Abel's offering greater value was his faith, not the fact that it was an animal sacrifice. Abel obtained this favor from God because his heart was purified by faith and only "faith" must inspire any worship that God will accept *"God testifying of his gifs,"* He confirms that no works, coming from us can please God, until we ourselves are received into favor. No works are deemed just before God, but those of a just man: for he reasons thus, God bore a testimony to Abel's gifts; then he had obtained the praise of being just before God. God, who regards only the inward purity of the heart, heeds not the outward masks of works. Therefore, no right or good work can proceed from us, until we are justified before God.

"By it he being dead," To faith he also ascribes this, that God testified that Abel was no less the object of his care after his death, than during his life. For when he says, that though dead, he still speaketh, he means, as Moses tells us, that God was moved by his violent death to take vengeance. "By which," and "by it," are commonly referred to faith, but the passage would be plainer, by

referring them to "the sacrifice." It was by the means or medium of the sacrifice, that the testimony was given, and it was on the account of it that Abel was put to death; "and through it, having died, he yet speaketh;" that is, though he died, owing to his sacrifice being approved, he yet speaketh, that is, by his example as a believer, say some, in the atonement; as a sufferer in behalf of the truth, say others. When Abel or his blood is said to speak, the words are to be understood figuratively. It was yet a singular evidence of God's love towards him, that he had a care for him even when he was dead.

3. Faith is necessary to please God (11:5-6)

"By faith Enoch was translated," (vs. 5) The author teaches us that through faith; it was that Enoch was translated. But we ought especially to consider the reason why God in so unusual a manner removed him from the earth. It was not to then an ordinary honor with which God had favored him. Moses indeed tells us, that he was a righteous man, and that he walked with God; but as righteousness begins with faith, it is justly ascribed to his faith, that he pleased God. "He reasons thus: — He who pleases God is endued with faith; Enoch pleased God; then Enoch was endued with faith." — J. Capellus. As to the subtle questions which the curious usually moot, it is better to pass them over, without taking much notice of them. They ask, what became of these two men, Enoch and Elijah? And then, that they

may not appear merely to ask questions, they imagine that they are reserved for the last days of the Church, that they may then come forth into the world; and for this purpose the Revelation of John is referred to. Let it suffice us to know, that their translation was a sort of extraordinary death; nor let us doubt but that they were divested of their mortal and corruptible flesh, in order that they might, with the other members of Christ, be renewed into a blessed immortality.

"But without faith it is impossible to please him,"(vs. 6) *But* there is no better interpreter than the author himself. The reason he assigns why no one can please God without faith, is because no one will ever come to God, except he believes that God is, and is also convinced that he is a remunerator to all who seek him. If access then to God is not opened, but by faith, it follows, that all that are without it, are the objects of God's disapproval. The author shows how faith obtains favor for us to the true worship of God, and makes us certain as to his goodwill, so that we may not think that we seek him in vain. These two clauses ought not to be slightly passed over, that we must believe that God is, and that we ought to feel assured that he is not sought in vain.

4. Heir of the Righteousness by Faith (11:7)

"By faith Noah," (vs. 7) Noah by faith prepared for things to come (by building "an ark").He did not live for the present. Noah wearied himself for a hundred and

twenty years in building the ark, that he stood unshaken amidst the scoffs of so many ungodly men, that he entertained no doubt but that he would be safe in the midst of the ruin of the whole world, yea, that he felt sure of life as it were in the grave, even in the ark. By continuing to believe the promises of God, even when everyone else disbelieved them, Noah inherited a new world after the Flood. The author had promised the readers "the world to come." (2:5-8) Noah's faith led to the preservation ("salvation") of his family ("household") similarly, as we continue to have faith in God, we will encourage others to do so, and they also will enter into their full inheritance if they follow our example of faithful perseverance. *"By which he condemned the world,"* And he is said on two accounts to have by the ark condemned the world; for by being so long occupied in building it, he took away every excuse from the wicked. The ark was made the means of deliverance to one family and the Lord wanted to spare a righteous man that he should not perish with the ungodly. Had he then not been preserved, the condemnation of the world would not have been so apparent. Noah then by obeying God's command condemned by his example the stubborn disobedience of the world. His wonderful deliverance from the midst of death was evidence that the world justly perished; for God would have doubtless saved it, had it not been unworthy of salvation. *"Of the righteousness which is by faith,"* This is the last thing in the character of Noah, which the author reminds us to observe. Faith rather than merely static belief spurs one to act in accordance with God's truth. The great people of faith have boldness and are backed up by the unseen; they step forward with confidence and with no observable reason for doing so. But God has spoken. So we are also called to an active faith that finds its reason in an unseen God.

5. The Doctrine of Faith (11:8-12)

From verse 8 to the end of the chapter, the Holy Spirit gives us fuller details concerning the life of faith, viewing it from different angles, contemplating varied aspects, and exhibiting the different trials to which it is subject and the blessed triumphs which Divine grace enables it to achieve. Fitly does this new section of our chapter open by presenting to us the case of Abraham. *"By faith Abraham, when he was called to go out,"* (vs. 8) *In* his days a new and important era of human history commenced. From this point onwards God's dealings with men were virtually confined to Abraham and his posterity. Abraham is designated "the *father* of all them that believe" (Rom. 4:11), which means not only that he is (as it were) the earthly head of the whole election of grace, but the one after whose likeness his spiritual children are conformed. There is a family likeness between Abraham and the true Christian, for if we are Christ's then are we "Abraham's seed and heirs according to promise" (Gal. 3:29), for "they which are of faith, the same are the children of Abraham" (Gal. 3:7), which is evidenced by them doing "the works of Abraham" (John 8:39), for these are the marks of identification.

The "fatherhood of Abraham" is twofold: natural, as the progenitor of a physical seed; spiritual, as the pattern to which his children are morally conformed. "By faith Abraham, when he was called to go out into a place which he should after receive for an inheritance, obeyed; and he went out, not knowing whither he went." (vs. 8)

True Faith is action taken in response to the unseen God and His promises. *"When he was called to go out into a place,"* To the command was added a promise, that God would give him a land for an inheritance. This promise he immediately embraced, and hastened as though he was sent to take possession of this land. This is differently connected by Calvin, his version is "by faith Abraham, when he was called, obeyed, so that he went forth," etc. Bloomfield by supposing [ωστε] understood before [ἐξελθεῖν], seems to be of the same opinion. Beza renders the verb by a gerund, ["abiendo]," by departing. This construction is more agreeable to the location of the words; the other introduces an unnatural transposition. There are thus two things in the verse stated more directly, as evidences and proofs of faith, his departure from his own country, and his ignorance as to the country where he was going. His faith was such that he obeyed, so as to leave his own country, and also to go to a country, of which he knew nothing. It is a no ordinary trial of faith to give up what we have in hand, in order to seek what is afar off, and unknown to us. For when God commanded him to leave his own country, he did not point out the place where he intended him to live, but left him in suspense and perplexity of mind: "go", he said, "into the place that I will show thee." (Genesis 12:1) The love of his native land might not only have retarded the promptness of Abraham, but also held him so bound to it, so as not to quit his home. His faith then was not of an ordinary kind, which thus broke through all hindrances and carried him where the Lord called him to go.

"By faith he sojourned in the land," (vs. 9) *The* second particular is, that having entered into the land, he was hardly received as a stranger and a sojourner. Where was the inheritance which he had expected? It might have indeed occurred instantly to his mind, that he had been deceived by God. Still greater was the disappointment, which the author does not mention, when shortly after a famine drove him from the country, when he was compelled to flee to the land of Gerar; but he considered it enough to say, as a commendation to his faith, that he became a sojourner in the land of promise; for to be a sojourner seemed contrary to what had been promised. Abraham boldly sustained this trial as an instance of

great fortitude that proceeded from faith alone. *"With Isaac and Jacob,"* The author does not mean that they dwelt in the same tent, or lived at the same time. He makes Abraham's son and grandson his companions, because they sojourned alike in the inheritance promised to them and yet failed not in their faith. The preposition μετὰ may often be rendered "as well as." (Matthew 2:3; Luke 11:7; 1 Corinthians 16:11) "Dwelling in tents, as well as Isaac and Jacob, co-heirs to the same promise," It means not here the same time, says Grotius, but parity as to what is stated. However long it was that God delayed the time; for the longer the delay the greater was the trial; but by setting up the shield of faith they repelled all the assaults of doubt and unbelief.

"For he looked for a city," (vs. 10) He gives a reason why he ascribes their patience to faith for they looked forward to heaven. This was indeed to see things invisible. It was no doubt a great thing to cherish in their hearts the assurance given them by God respecting the possession of the land until it was after some ages realized. They did not confine their thoughts to that land, but penetrated even into heaven, it was still a clearer evidence of their faith. He calls heaven a *city that has foundations,* because of its eternity since in the world there is transitory and fading. It may indeed appear strange that he makes God the Maker of heavens as though he did not also create the earth. The words, "builder and maker," are rendered by Calvin, "master

builder and maker." The first word means the maker or worker; and the second, the master-builder or planner. The order is, according to what is very common in Scripture, the effect mentioned first, then the cause, of the maker first, then the contriver. The last word, no doubt used in the sense of a worker or maker, but also in the sense of an architect or planner; but the former word means a skillful worker or artificer, but not a master-builder. In order, therefore, to give a meaning to each, the sentence is to be thus rendered, "Whose maker and planner is God;" he not only made it, but also planned and contrived it. Whatever is formed by men is like its authors in instability; so also is the perpetuity of the heavenly life, it corresponds with the nature of God its founder. Moreover, the Apostle teaches us that all weariness is relieved by expectation, so that we ought never to be weary in following God.

"Through faith also, Sarah herself," (vs. 11) *The* author challenges women to know that this truth belongs to them as well as to men. He gives the example of Sarah; which he mentions in preference to that of others for she was the mother of all the faithful. It must indeed be confessed, that her faith was blended with unbelief; but as she cast aside her unbelief when reproved, her faith is acknowledged by God and commended. What then she rejected at first as being incredible, she afterwards as soon as she heard that it came from God, obediently received.

"Because she judged him faithful," Were any one only to hear that Sarah brought forth a child through faith, all that is meant would not be conveyed to him, but the explanation which the Apostle adds removes every obscurity; for he declares that Sarah's faith was this, that she counted God to be true to his word, that is, to what he had promised. Consequently, Sarah is said to have counted God faithful who had promised. True faith then is that which hears God speaking and rests on his promise.

"Therefore sprang there even of one,"(vs. 12) The author reminds these Hebrews that it was by faith that they were the descendants of Abraham; for he was as it were half dead and Sarah his wife, who had been barren in the flower of her age, was now sterile, being far advanced in years. Calvin renders ταῦτα adverbially "quidem," "and indeed dead;" Doddridge "in his repeat;" Macknight, "to these matters;" Stuart "as to these things." But the word is rendered in Luke 6:23, "in the like manner;" and this would be the best rendering here. Abraham was like Sarah, "dead" as to the power of begetting children, "Therefore even from one, and him in a like manner dead, there sprang so many as the stars."

6. The Perseverance of Faith (11:13-16)

"These all died in faith,"(vs. 13) He enhances by a comparison the faith of the patriarchs: for when they had

only tasted of the promises, as though fully satisfied with their sweetness, they despised all that was in the world; and they never forgot the taste of them, however small it was either in life or in death. The phrase *"in faith"* is differently explained. Some say that they died in faith, because in this life they never enjoyed the promised blessings. Just as currently, salvation is hid from us, being hoped for. "Though God gave to the fathers only a taste of that grace which is largely poured on us, though he showed to them at a distance only an obscure representation of Christ, who is now set forth to us clearly before our eyes, yet they were satisfied and never fell away from their faith: how much greater reason then have we at this day to persevere? If we grow faint, we are doubly inexcusable". It is then an enhancing circumstance, that the fathers had a distant view of the spiritual kingdom of Christ. Hence it is that though they had the same salvation promised them, yet they had not the promises so clearly revealed to them as they are to us under the kingdom of Christ; but they were content to behold them afar off. *"And confessed that they were strangers,"* Jacob, when he answered Pharaoh, that the time of his pilgrimage was short compared with that of his fathers, and full of many sorrows (Genesis 47:9) confessed himself a pilgrim in the land, which had been promised to him as a perpetual inheritance. It is quite evident that his mind was by no means fixed on this world, but that he raised it up above the heavens. The author concludes that the fathers, by speaking openly showed that they had a better country in heaven; for as they were pilgrims here, they had a country and an abiding habitation elsewhere. *"Wherefore God is not ashamed,"* (vs. 16) *The* author now refers to that passage, "I am the God of Abraham, the God of Isaac, and the God of Jacob" (Exodus 3:6). It is a singular honor when God makes men well-known, by attaching his name to them. The author teaches us to depend on faith. There will be for us no inheritance in heaven, except we become pilgrims on earth; However, he concludes with these words, "I am the God of Abraham, of Isaac, and of Jacob," that they were heirs of heaven, since he who thus speaks is not the God of the dead, but of the living.

7. The Faith of Abraham in Sacrificing Isaac (11:17-19)

"By faith Abraham," (vs. 17) *The* author proceeds with the history of Abraham, and relates the offering up of his son which was a singular instance of steadfastness."We are apt to see this as a conflict between Abraham's love for his son and his duty to God. But for the author the problem was Abraham's difficulty in reconciling the different revelations made to him."[19] For the sake of enhancing it, he further says *when he was tempted,* or

---

[19]Morris, pp. 121-22.

tried. Abraham had previously proved what he was, by many trials; nevertheless this trial seemed to be more than other trials. When we look at the lives of the heroes of faith like Abraham, each one had weaknesses and shortcomings. They are heroes not because they were perfect before God but because they worked with God in His perfect plan.

The word, *tempted* or *tried*, means proved. The sacrificing of Isaac is to be anticipated according to the purpose of the heart because his decision to obey God was then the same, as though he had actually sacrificed his son. *"And he that received the promises,"* All the promises that God gave Abraham were founded on this pronouncement, "In Isaac shall thy seed be called," (Genesis 21:12)[20] for when this foundation was taken away, no hope of blessing or of grace remained. And yet by faith he emerged above all these thoughts, so as to accomplish what he was commanded. How it is that Abraham's faith is praised when it departs from the

---

[20] The words literally are "In Isaac shall be called to thee a seed." But the Hebrew and the Greek ἐν, mean often by or through, or by the means of: and the Hebrew verb, to be called, as well as the Greek, may sometimes be rendered to be. Hence Macknight seems to have been right in his version of the clause, "By Isaac a seed shall be thee;" which is better than that of Stuart, "After Isaac shall thy seed be named," for this is less literal, and the meaning is not conveyed.

promise? For as obedience proceeds from faith, so faith from the promise; then when Abraham was without the promise, his faith must have fallen to the ground. Abraham was willing to continue to trust and obey God, illustrated when he "offered up Isaac," because he believed God could even "raise" Isaac, his unique (Gr. monogenes) son, "from the dead" to fulfil His promises of an heir. Similarly, we need to continue to trust and obey God even though He may have to raise us from the dead to fulfil His promises to us. Isaac's restoration was "a type" (Gr. parabole , parable, figure, illustration) of the fact that God will give us what He has promised if we continue to trust and obey Him. When Isaac arose from the altar, it was just as if he had risen from the dead.But the death of Isaac must have been the death of all the promises; for Isaac is not to be considered as a common man, but as one who had Christ included in him. Abraham approved this honor to God, that he was able to raise his son Isaac again from the dead. Therefore, he did not forsake the promise given to him but he instead extended its power and its truth beyond the life of his son; for he did not limit God's power to so narrow bounds as to tie it to Isaac when dead. *"Offered up his only begotten son,"* Here the author is trying to show how great the trial of Abraham was. Abraham was commanded to take his only begotten and beloved son Isaac, to sacrifice him with his own hands. God commanded him to go a three days' journey. The death of a son must have been very grievous, a bloody death would have caused greater sorrow; and must have been too dreadful for a father's heart to endure.

"From whence also," (vs. 19) although Isaac did not really rise from the dead, he seemed to have in a way risen from death, when God magnificently rescued him. [21] That sacrifice was a representation of Christ. Abraham did not receive his Son otherwise than if he had been restored from death to new life.

---

[21] The meaning given by Stuart and some others is very far fetched, though said to be natural, that "Abraham believed that God could raise Isaac from the dead, because he had, as it were, obtained him from the dead, i.e., he was born of those who were dead as to these things." Hence the rendering given is "comparatively." Abraham had, as to his purpose, sacrificed him, so that he considered him as dead; and he received him back from the dead, not really, but in a way bearing a likeness to such a miracle. This sense is alone compatible with the former clause, which mentions Abraham's faith in God's power to raise his son from the dead; he believed that God was able to do this; and then it is added that Abraham had received back his son as though he had sacrificed him, and as though God had raised him from the dead. What actually took place bore a likeness to the way which he had anticipated. Costallio gives the meaning, "it was the same as though he had sacrificed him, and received him also in a manner he received him."

8. The Faith of Isaac and Jacob (11:20-22)

"By faith Isaac," (vs. 20) The blessing of Isaac was very different; for it was as it were an introduction into the possession of the land, which God had promised to him and his posterity. We see that this blessing depended on faith; for Isaac had nothing which he could have bestowed on his children but the word of God (Genesis 27:29) It may, however, be doubted whether there was any faith in the blessing given to Esau, as he was a reprobate and rejected by God. Faith mainly shone forth, when he distinguished between the two twins born to him, so that he gave the first place to the younger; for following the oracle of God, he took away from the firstborn the ordinary right of nature. And on this depended the condition of the whole nation of Israel, that Jacob was chosen by God, and that this choice was approved by the blessing of the father.

"By faith Jacob," (vs. 21) For the tribe of Ephraim was so superior to the rest that they in a manner did lie down under its shade; for the Scripture often includes the ten tribes under this name. And Ephraim was the younger of the two sons of Joseph, and when Jacob blessed him and his brother, they were both young. What did Jacob observe in the younger, to prefer him to the first born? His eyes were dim with age so that he could not see, but he laid his right hand by chance on the head of Ephraim, but he crossed his hands, so that he moved his right hand to the left side. He assigned to them two portions, as

though he was now the Lord of that land, from which famine had driven him away.

"By faith Joseph," (vs. 22) Joseph had shown faith by ordering his bones to be exported; he had no regard to himself, as though his grave in the land of Canaan would be sweeter or better than in Egypt.After he suffered so much in his life, as he was about to die, he showed his faith by prophesying Israel's departure and requiring that his bones be taken when they left. (Genesis 50:24, 25; Exodus 13:19) But his main aim was to sharpen the yearning of his own nation that they might more solemnly seek after redemption. He also wished to strengthen their faith so that they might boldly hope that they would be delivered.

9. The Faith of Moses` parents (11:23-26)

"By faith Moses when he was born, was hid three months of his parents,"(vs. 23) The Egyptians had been kind to the Hebrews at the time of Joseph by giving them the land of Goshen to dwell in. Then another king arose who "knew not Joseph" perhaps a foreigner who had conquered Egypt. This new king oppressed the descendants of Abraham and this new ruler of Egypt quickly became apparent: "And he said unto his people, Behold, the people of the children of Israel are more and mightier than we: come on, let us deal wisely with them, lest they multiply, and it come to pass, that when there falleth out any war, they join also unto our enemies."

(Ex. 1:9, 10) So it proved here, for "the more they afflicted them, the more they multiplied and grew" (Ex. 1:12). Then, the king of Egypt gave orders to the midwives that every male child of the Hebrews should be slain at birth. (Ex. 1:15, 16) Faith confronted hostility in a characteristic way that the writer began to emphasize in this verse. Amram and Jochebed's faith in God, in their placing His wills above Pharaoh's command. (They perseveringly hid Moses for three months" and "were not afraid of the king's edict") Moses was not an ordinary child, among other ways, in that his parents saved his life even though Pharaoh had ordered all Jewish male babies killed. Josephus wrote that Moses was an unusually beautiful (Heb. tob) baby.[22] "But all the laws which men may make against the promises that God has given to His church, are doomed to certain failure. God had promised unto Abraham a numerous "seed" (Gen. 13:15), and had declared to Jacob, "fear not to go down into Egypt, for I will there make of thee a great nation" (Gen. 46:3); as well, then, might Pharaoh attempt to stop the sun from shining as prevent the growth of the children of Israel. (Ex. 1:17). Refusing to accept defeat, "Pharaoh charged all his people, saying, every son that is born ye shall cast into the river." (Ex. 1:22)

"By faith Moses, when he was come to years," (vs. 24) Through Moses, the Jews were delivered from bondage

---

[22]Josephus, Antiquities of …, 2:9:6.

in Egypt and the covenant of God was renewed. But if faith is to be considered as the main thing in Moses' life, it would be very strange that he should draw them away to anything else. When he grew up, he disregarded the adoption of Pharaoh's daughter. That we may then know that nothing was done thoughtlessly, and without a long deliberation, the author says, that he was of mature age, which is also evident from history. [23]

But he is said to have disregarded his adoption; for when he visited his brethren, when he tried to relieve them, when he avenged their wrongs, he fully proved that he preferred to return to his own people, rather than to remain in the king's court. This was an act of faith; for it would have been much better for him to remain in Egypt, had he not been persuaded of the blessing promised to the race of Abraham; and of this blessing,

---

23 Literally it is "when he became great," that is, in age or in years: he was, as it appears from Acts 7:23, about forty years of age. The word "great," both in Hebrew and Greek, has sometimes this meaning. "When arrived at mature age," by Stuart, is better than "when he was grown up," by Doddridge and Macknight. It is said that he refused, that is by his conduct. He acted in such a way as to show that he rejected the honor of being adopted son of Pharoah's daughter. The verb means to deny, to renounce, to disown. He renounced the privilege offered to him. Others are said to "deny the power" of godliness, that is by their works. 2 Timothy 3:5.

the only witness was God's promise; for he could see nothing of the kind with his eyes.

"Esteeming the reproach of Christ greater riches," (vs. 26) *When* Moses became an adult, he refused to benefit from the privileges associated with being "the son of Pharaoh's daughter." He turned his back on the world and all that it offered him. Instead, he chose to suffer affliction with the Hebrews because they were "the people of God," not because they were the people of Israel, or his people. (vs. 25) Moses had a true appreciation for the promises of God. This led him to choose the reward associated with Israel's promised Messiah reproach of Christ over "greater riches than" the temporary material wealth "passing pleasures" and "treasures" he could have enjoyed had he stayed in "Egypt."He was laying up treasure in heaven.[24] We ourselves should be willing to suffer temporary disgrace, reproach, and loss, as we continue to cast our lot with God's faithful disciples. *"For he had respect unto the recompense of the reward,"* The high-mindedness of Moses was owing to faith; for he had his eyes fixed on the promise of God. By Faith, Moses hoped that it would be better for him to be with the people of Israel than with the Egyptians.

More than this, our decisions should be motivated by the expectation of receiving rewards. ... The author is

---

[24]Robertson, 5:426.

encouraging the Hebrews not to live for what the world will promise you them but for what God has promised them. "The prospect of reward is the most commonly mentioned motivation for enduring in the faith."

10. The Faith of Moses (11:27-29)

"By faith he forsook Egypt," (vs. 27) Moses definitely left Egypt when he fled from the house of Pharaoh. Despite the king's "wrath," Moses persevered and departed (left Egypt) for Midian, 40 years before the exodus is in view here. The reference to the king's "wrath" is appropriate, because Moses left Egypt on the occasion when Pharaoh wanted to kill him but (Exod. 2:15) it was not personal fear of Pharaoh but the awareness of his destiny as the deliverer of the covenant people that caused him to take flight. Had he remained [in Egypt], at that juncture, this destiny would have been thwarted, humanly speaking, by his execution; and so, impelled by faith in the divine purpose for his life, Moses took refuge in Midian."[25]

"As seeing him who is invisible," God at that time only showed him a certain symbol of his presence; but he was far from seeing God as he is. The reference is not to the awesome event at the burning bush ..., as if to say that

---

[25]4P. E. Hughes, A Commentary ..., p. 499. Cf. Dods, 4:361.

Moses saw one who is invisible, but to a fixed habit of spiritual perception. ...God appeared to Moses in such a way, as still to leave room for faith. When he overwhelmed by terrors on every side, he turned all his thoughts to God. He was indeed assisted to do this, by the vision which we have mentioned; but yet he saw more in God than what that symbol intimated: for he understood his power.

"Through faith he kept the Passover," (vs. 28) The Israelites held this first sacrifice of the Passover in the highest esteem. They were to slay lambs and sprinkle their blood on the doorposts and lintels of their houses. Then they were to eat a feast, as God directed, ready to leave the land. God then destroyed the firstborn in all the homes having no blood on the door, but the Israelite sons were spared. Pharaoh then demanded that the Israelites leave. The author here records simply Moses' faith, because he trusted in God's word alone. And the reason why he mentions Moses alone, as celebrating the Passover, seems to be this, that God through him instituted the Passover.

"By faith they passed," (vs. 29) *Many* Israelites were unbelieving; but God gave faith to the few, that the whole multitude should pass through the Red Sea on dry land. The Israelites experienced victory over their enemies as they trusted God. At the "Red Sea," the Israelites willingly went forward at God's word ("passed

through"), rather than turning back but their enemies perished in the Red Sea. Trust and obedience resulted in the Israelites' preservation. The Israelites were preserved safe, because they relied on God's word.

"By faith the walls of Jericho fell," (vs. 30) By faith the Israelites gained the possession of the Promised Land. For at their first entrance the city Jericho stood in their way; it being fortified and almost impenetrable, it impeded any farther progress, and they had no means to assail it. The Lord commanded them to go round it once every day and on the seventh day seven times. It is evident, that the walls did not fall through the shout of men or the sound of trumpets; but because the people believed that the Lord would do what he had promised. Therefore, by faith the walls of Jericho fell down, and they ultimately entered into their inheritance. In the same way, by faith, we can be freed from the domination of the Devil and brought to liberty, we can put to flight all our enemies, and all the strongholds of hell can be demolished.

"By faith the harlot Rahab," (vs. 31) The story of Rahab is told in Joshua chapter 2. Rahab was a harlot living in Jericho. As Israel arrived to fight the city, they sent two spies into the city and the men of the city attempted to capture these spies, but Rahab hid them and helped them escape. She said she did so because she had heard of Israel's accomplishments and she believed God was with

them. (Verses 9-13) She begged them to spare her and her family, when they took the city.Moreover; James also bears testimony to the faith of Rahab. (James 2:25) She was endued with true faith; for she professed her full persuasion of what God had promised to the Israelites; and of those whom fear kept from entering the land. The evidence of her faith was that she received the spies at the peril of her life: then, by means of faith, she escaped safe from the ruin of her own city. She is mentioned as a *harlot,* in order to amplify the grace of God.[26] But such a fear was groundless; for in the history of Joshua, this word, and harlot, is expressly added, in order that we may know that the spies came into the city Jericho clandestinely, and concealed themselves in a harlot's house. At the same time this must be understood of her past life; for faith is an evidence of repentance.

11. Other Heroes of Faith (11:32-34)

"And what shall I say more?"(vs. 32) The author has listed and briefly summarized the works of faith of several Old Testament characters. He now summarizes numerous others, saying that he did not have time to tell about them. Since his purpose did not require giving

---

26 And it has been adopted by many of the German divines, who seem in many instances to follow any vagary, Rabbinical or heathen, rather than the word of God. There is nothing in Scripture that countenances this notion. The word is never used in the sense of a hostess: and the ancient versions ever render the Hebrew word by πόρνη, a harlot.

detail, then we will not take time to discuss them in detail either. He first refers to the time that intervened between Joshua and David, when the Lord had raised up judges to govern the people; and such were the four he now mentions, Gideon, Barak, Samson, and Jephthah. It amazing that through Gideon, God used only three hundred men to attack a huge host of enemies and to shake pitchers appeared like a sham alarm. Barak was far inferior to his enemies, and was guided only by the counsel of a woman. Samson was a mere countryman, who had never used any other arms than the implements of husbandry. What could he do against such proved conquerors, by whose power the whole people had been subdued? Who would not at first have condemned the rashness of Jephthah, who declared himself the avenger of a people already past hope? But as they all followed the guidance of God, and being animated by his promise, undertook what was commanded them, they have been honored with the testimony of the Holy Spirit.[27] Then the author ascribes all that was commendable in them to

27 The history of Gideon we have in Judges 6:11, to the end of the 8th chapter: of Barak, in Judges 4:6, to the end of the 5th: of Samson, in Judges 13:24, to the end of the 16th: and of Jephthah, in Judges 11:1, to the end of the 12th chapter. Thus we see that the order of time in which they lived is not here observed, it being not necessary for the object of the author. Barak was before Gideon, Jephthah before Samson, and Samuel before David.

faith although there was no one of them whose faith did not halt. *Gideon* was not slower to take up arms than what he ought to have been or did he attempt to commit himself to God. *Barak* at first trembled, so that he was almost forced by the reproofs of Deborah. *Samson* being overcome by the blandishments of a concubine ignorantly betrayed the safety of the whole people. *Jephthah*, hasty in making a foolish vow, and too determined in performing it, blemished the finest victory by the cruel death of his own daughter. Therefore, in all these heroes, something at fault is ever to be found; yet faith, though hesitant and imperfect, is still approved by God. Under David's name he includes all the pious kings, and to them he adds *Samuel* and the *Prophets.* The many victories of David, which he had gained over his enemies, were commonly known. Known also, was the uprightness of Samuel, and his consummate wisdom in governing the people. Known too were the great favors conferred by God on prophets and kings.

It was by faith that David so many times returned home as a conqueror; that Hezekiah recovered from his sickness; that Daniel came forth safe and untouched from the lions' den, and that his friends walked in a burning furnace as cheerfully as on a pleasant field. Since all these things were done by faith, we must feel convinced, that in no other way than by faith is God's goodness and bounty to be communicated to us.

"Who through faith subdued kingdoms," (vs. 33) This was done by Joshua, Gideon, and many of the judges listed, as well as by David. Many unnamed men of faith did likewise. *"They wrought righteousness,"* Faith leads to active obedience to God's will. But true faith that pleases God always expresses itself in righteous living, and no one is rewarded before or without such works. This chapter of faith does not maintain the doctrine of faith only. In fact, it is one of the most powerful proofs that we are saved by faith, but not by faith without obedience. They also *"obtained promises,"* They obtained blessings that God promised to them, but they obtained them on the condition of obedient faith alone. Specific promises would include the ones to Abraham, Noah, David, etc. *"Stopped lions' mouths,"* This was done by Daniel (Daniel 6). David also defeated lions (1 Samuel 17:34, 35), as did Samson (Judges 14:5, 6). These too are taken as evidence of faith, but all concerned active obedience.

"Quenched fire," (vs. 34) This is the case of the three friends Shadrach, Meshach, and Abednego. (Daniel 3) They were thrown in to a fiery furnace because they refused to bow to Nebuchadnezzar's image. Yet God spared them from the fire. *"Escaped the edge of the sword,"* This would apply to nearly all who were involved in battles: David, Joshua, and many of the judges. *"Out of weakness were made strong,"*Chrysostom refers this to the restoration of the

Jews from exile, in which they were like men without hope; I do not disapprove of its applications to Hezekiah. We might at the same time extend it wider, that the Lord, by his hand, raised on high his saints, whenever they were cast down; and brought help to their weakness, so as to endure them with full strength. This would include childless Abraham and Sarah who yet became the source of a huge nation, Gideon with his 300 men, Daniel in the lion's den, and his three friends in the fiery furnace, etc. Faith leads us to strive to achieve apparently impossible goals, simply because God says so. Do we have that faith?

12. The Heroes of Faith Tested in Hardships (11:35-40)

"Women received theirdead raised to life again," (vs. 35) There were miracles in the Old Testament of the dead being raised to life as well as in the New Testament. It was done by God both through Elijah and Elisha (1 Kings 17:17-24; 2 Kings 4:17-37). Some suffered at great length at the hands of their enemies. They might have escaped had they been willing to compromise their stand for truth, but they knew there was a better life if they would serve God. Examples would include Jeremiah (38:5ff), Daniel, and his three friends. In fact, such treatment was so common of Old Testament prophets that Stephen, in Acts 7:52, asked which of the prophets the people did not persecute!

(Matthew 23:30-37). This phrase raises the interesting idea that belief in resurrection existed in Old Testament times. (Hosea 13:14). During the time of Jesus, Pharisees defended the resurrection and Sadducees denied it. Jesus strongly defended it, even from the Old Testament, yet Old Testament references to it are not many. The doctrine is clearly stated and defended in the New Testament. (Acts 24:15; Luke 20:27-39; John 6:40-45; 5:21-29; 1 Corinthians 15:12-58; 6:14; 2 Corinthians 4:14; 1 Thessalonians 4:13-18) *"Women received,"* "Women received back their dead" because they believed God could and would do what He had promised. (cf. 1 Kings 17:17-24; 2 Kings 4:17-37) *"Others were tortured"*, As to this verb, [ἐτυμπανίσθησαν], I have followed Erasmus, though others render it "imprisoned." But the simple meaning is, as I think, that they were stretched on a rack, as the skin of a drum, which is distended. [28] By saying that they were tempted, he seems to have spoken what was

---

28 The τύμπανον was, according to Schleusner, a machine on which the body was stretched; and then cudgels or rods, and whips were used. This appears from the account given in 2 Macc. 6: 19, 30. It is said that Eleasar, rather than transgress the Law, went of his own accord "to the torment" — ἐπὶ τὸ τύμπανον, and in the 30th verse mention is made of stripes or strokes — πληγαῖς, and of being lashed or whipped — μαστιγούμενος. This was to be tympanized or tortured.

202

superfluous; and I doubt not but that the likeness of the words, [ἐπρίσθησαν] and [ἐπειράσθησαν], was the reason that the word was added by some unskillful transcriber, and thus crept into the text, as also Erasmus has conjectured. Now though they say that Jeremiah was stoned, that Isaiah was sawn asunder, and though sacred history relates that Elijah, Elisha, and other Prophets, wandered on mountains and in caves. Here the author may be pointing out those persecutions which Antiochus carried against God's people.

"Not accepting deliverance," That they might then live forever in heaven, they rejected a life on earth, which would have cost them, as we have said, so much as the denial of God, and also the repudiation of their own calling. The "better resurrection" that those who were tortured, but did not accept their release obtained, was perhaps their bodily resurrection, in contrast to the "resurrection" from reproach to honour, from poverty to riches, from pain to ease and pleasure that they could have obtained by apostatizing.Moreover, by this verse the author confirms what he had said, that the saints overcome all sufferings by faith; for except their minds had been sustained by the hope of a blessed resurrection, they must have immediately failed.

"Of whom the world was not worthy," (vs. 38) As the holy Prophets wandered as fugitives among wild beasts, they might have seemed unworthy of being sustained on

the earth; for how was it that they could find no place among men? But the author says that the world was not worthy of them; for wherever God's servants come, they bring with them his blessing like the fragrance of a sweet odor. The house of Potiphar was blessed for Joseph's sake, (Genesis 39:5) and Sodom would have been spared had ten righteous men been found in it (Genesis 18:32).

"And these all,"(vs. 39) having obtained a good report through faith, have not received the promise. God foreordained as to us something more excellent, so that they without us might not be perfected." The faithful heroes that died in Old Testament times have not yet entered into their inheritances. This awaits the Second Coming when Christ will resurrect and judge Old Testament saints. (Dan. 12:1-2; cf. Isa. 26:19) We will have some part in their reward and apart from us they would not be made perfect. We will at least do so as Christ's companions who will witness their award ceremony. Their being "made perfect" refers to their entering into their final "rest" (inheritance), and it rests entirely, as ours does, on the sacrificial death of Christ. (cf. 9:15) What more could any of us desire, than that in all the blessings which God bestowed on Abraham, Moses, David, and all the Patriarchs, on the Prophets and godly kings, he should have a regard for us, so that we might be united together with them in the body of Christ? By the words, that *they received not the promise* is to be understood its ultimate fulfillment, which took

place in Christ, on which subject something has been said already.

The phrase *"some better thing"* (vs. 40) is considered to be the same with the promise, or to be the Gospel as revealed, or in the words of Stuart, "the actual fulfillment of the promise respecting the Messiah." "The better thing" is the atoning death of Christ, which was to the ancient saints an unfulfilled event, but to us fulfilled and clearly revealed, and yet its benefits extended to them as well as to us. The "promise" throughout this letter is that of "the eternal inheritance" and "the promises" in verse 13 include this and others, and especially "the better things," that is the Gospel, or fulfillment of what was necessary to attain the inheritance, even the death and resurrection of Christ; or we may say that it is "the better hope," (chapter 7:19) or the "better covenant, which was established on better promises." (Chapter 8:6)

Hebrews 12

C. Things that Encourage Faithfulness (chapter 12)

1. Running the Race (12:1-4)

"Wherefore seeing we also are compassed," (vs. 1) *The* author applies different illustrations given in the previous chapter, making use of them as a grand motive to perseverance in the Christian faith and state. Analysing the particular terms of our text, we find there is, first, the duty enjoined: to "run the race that is set before us." Second, the obstacles to be overcome: "lay aside every weight" etc. Third, the fundamental grace which is required thereto: "patience." Fourth, the encouragement given: the "great cloud of witnesses." The author begins the chapter with the familiar Race metaphor and presents a forceful challenge to Christians to endure in a marathon commitment to Christ. The author joins chapter 11 and 12 with the term "therefore. "The author employs the metaphor 'cloud' pointing back

to the multitudes of persons listed or alluded to in chapter 11 as "such a great cloud". These great characters of faith from the Old Testament become witnesses to us, so many in numbers that they are called a great cloud of witnesses. As witnesses, they testify to us of the value of faith and the benefit it can have in our relationship to God, especially regarding salvation. *Cloud of witnesses* means that the countless thousands of God's faithful throughout the ages now sit in the stands of eternity, observing Christians as they seek to live for Christ in the world. The "cloud of witnesses" refers to the Old Covenant saints whom the writer just mentioned. (ch. 11) The preceding chapter presented them as bearing witness to their faith. The description of these predecessors as a "cloud" is an interesting one, since they are presently without resurrected bodies. They await the resurrection of their bodies at the Second Coming. (Dan 12:2) The word witness can carry the meaning 'spectator' or 'surrounded' and shows the ancient amphitheater with the tiered rows of seats. The faithful of the ages are witnesses in the sense that they bear witness to the Christian community of God's faithfulness and of the effectiveness of Faith. These Faithful followers offer motivation to the Christian community.

"If all the saints of God lived, suffered, endured, and conquered by faith, shall not we also? A Christian is likened unto an athlete, and his life unto the running of a race. This is one of a number of figures used in the N.T.

to describe the Christian life. "The author now returns to the duty of [hupomone]"endurance" as the immediate exercise of [pistis] "faith," as the great Believer, who shows us what true [pistis] means, from beginning to end, in its heroic course [ton prokeimenon heminagona] "the race that is set before us."Believers are likened to shining lights, branches of the vine, soldiers, strangers and pilgrims: the last-mentioned more closely resembling the figure employed in our text, but with this difference: travellers may rest for awhile, and refresh themselves, but the racer must *continue* running or he ceases to be a "racer." The figure of the race occurs frequently, both in the Old and New Testaments (Psalm 119:32, Song of Solomon 1:4, 1 Corinthians 9:24, Philippians 3:14, 2 Timothy 4:7).The main views suggested by the figure of the "race" are self-denial and discipline, enthusiastic hard work, and persevering endurance. The Christian life is of active *"fighting* the good fight of faith!" The Christian is not called to lie down on fancy beds of ease, but to run a race. Athletics are strenuous, demanding self-sacrifice, hard training, the putting forth of every ounce of energy possessed.The competition of Christian life is different from that of a race in two significant ways. First we compete by faith but not with each other. Our competition is against Satan, his world system and our own sinfulness. Second our strength is not in ourselves but in the Holy Spirit. *"Let us lay aside every weight,* or *every burden,"* One of the greatest problems Runners face is weight. "Encumbrances" are added weights (burdens), which may not necessarily be sins, but nevertheless make perseverance difficult. The Greek word translated "encumbrance" is [ogkos], which means [protuberance], A protuberance is a tumour or swelling, an excess growth. So the idea seems to be that we should lay aside anything that is superfluous, that we do not need, in order to run the race successfully. The author tells his hearers to throw off everything that hinders and the sin that so easily entangles. The weight so easily diverts our attention, saps our energy and dampens our enthusiasm for things of God. For Success one has to get rid of anything that would hinder breathing or the free movement of the limbs. So a Christian should lay aside everything if the faith race is to be run triumphantly.

We do not know exactly what kind of things the author had in mind regarding spiritual encumbrances and commentators venture a host of ideas. If the context of the letter is considered, the main encumbrance can be Judaistic legalism, hanging on to the old religious ways. The Jewish religious ways were sapping energy and attention from Christian living. So these were all weights and some of these were very heavy weights. Another type of weight can be fellow Christians. We need to be careful about blaming others for our mistakes. But some Christians not only are not running but also are keeping others from not running. The author writes here to lay aside every weight and to get rid of every *'entangling sin.'* We should also "lay aside … sin" of any kind. "The sin" that the writer warned his readers against especially in Hebrews is unbelief, apostasy. In view of the immediately preceding context, it might refer to "losing heart," "quitting the race," or "giving up the fight." However, many different kinds of sin can trip us up, and we should avoid all sin for this reason.The author does not seem to refer to a specific sin but rather as any sin hindering progress in the faith.

"Looking unto Jesus the author and finisher of our faith,"(vs. 2) The ultimate example showing what is required of us, though not mentioned in chapter 11, is Jesus. As a runner keeps looking toward the goal, so we should keep looking to Jesus. When we take our eyes of faith off Jesus, we begin to sink, like Peter did (Matt. 14:22-33). Jesus should be our primary model when it comes to persevering. The author used the name *"Jesus"* to accent our Lord's humanity, especially His endurance of pain, humiliation, and the disgrace of the cross. He is the author of the New Testament faith and the finisher (or "perfecter" – ASV, NASB, RSV) of it. We are called to fix our eyes on Jesus, the author and perfector of our own faith. He is our "author." (lit. "file leader," "captain," "pioneer" 2:10). It was by looking to Him in faith that we were saved. Jesus set the example of "living by faith" for us, one evidence of His faith being His prayers. Jesus perfected faith in the sense that He

finished His course of "living by faith" successfully (cf. 2:13).

As the 'perfector of faith' Jesus is the one in whom faith has reached its perfection. Looking to a King or Leader as a model for inspiration was common in those times. In the context of the 'Race' Jesus is the one who has run the race before us and he gives a good example of how the race is to be finished. He is the author and perfector of our faith. The word author is rich with meaning and gives the idea of a champion, leader, forerunner or initiator. The word has already been used in Hebrews in the context of Christ's bringing of salvation. (2:10) Both the concepts of forerunner and champion fit in this passage. *"Who for the joy that was set before him,"* Though the expression in Latin is somewhat ambiguous, yet according to the words in Greek the author's meaning is quite clear; for he intimates, that though it was free to Christ to exempt himself from all trouble and to lead a happy life, abounding in all good things, he yet underwent a death that was bitter, and in every way humiliating. For the expression, *for joy,* is the same as, instead of joy; and joy includes every kind of enjoyment. And he says, *set before him,* because the power of availing himself of this joy was possessed by Christ, had it so pleased him. At the same time if anyone thinks that the preposition [ἀντὶ] denotes the final cause, I do not much object; then the meaning would be that Christ refused not the death of the cross, because he saw its blessed issue. Jesus perfected faith and provided the preeminent example of endurance because he looked beyond immediate, painful circumstances to the reward that was ahead. The term 'scorn' means treating something as though it had little value. Jesus 'scorned' the shame of the cross means that he treated it as of little importance.

The author's words are very powerful here. The cross was the lowest form of capital punishment in the Roman world, reserved for slaves and criminals and involving torture and mocking. On the cross Jesus was treated as valueless being mocked and ridiculed. He compared the Cross insignificant compared to the joy set before our Lord. The end result of his shame was his exaltation to God's right hand. Thus Christian believers are encouraged to look beyond their present problems to God's promised reward.

"For consider him that endured," (vs. 3) he urges the readers to think upon "consider" Jesus, so they might not "grow weary" of persevering and "lose heart." Meditation on Jesus and the cross encourages us to continue to follow God's will faithfully. It is natural for us to overestimate the severity of our trials, and the writer did not want us to do this.

"Ye have not yet resisted unto blood," (vs. 4) Many of the Hebrew Christians to whom the Gospel was written had started well. They had seen signs and wonders and

were thrilled with their new lives. (2:4) But as the new began to wear off and problems began to arise, they began to lose their enthusiasm and confidence. They started looking back at the old customs of Judaism and around them at the persecution and suffering and they began to weaken and waver. One of the greatest motivations to the unbelieving Jews and the Christians would be all those great believers from the past, who lived a life of Faith.

He proceeds farther, for he reminds us, that even when the ungodly persecute us for Christ's sake, we are then contending against sin. The present state of the oppressed Hebrews is here expressed negatively:"ye have not yet resisted unto blood." True, they had already met with various forms of suffering, but not yet had they been called upon to lay down their lives. As Hebrews 10:32-34 clearly intimates, they had well acquitted themselves during the first stages of their trials, but their warfare was not yet ended. The author here hinted to the Hebrews what might yet have to be endured by them, namely a bloody and violent death probably by stoning, or the sword, or fire. The readers had "not yet resisted" sin to the extent that their enemies were torturing them, "shedding" their "blood," or killing them for their faith— as had been Jesus' experience.

Evidently there had been no martyrs among the readers yet, though the writer and the readers undoubtedly knew of Christians elsewhere who had died for their faith. (e.g., Stephen, James, et al.) Their "striving against sin" probably refers to both resisting sinful opponents and resisting inward temptations to sin in their own lives. (v. 1; cf. Luke 18:1; Gal.6:9) That is the extreme which brutal persecutors can afflict them. Those who serve under the banner of Christ, have no guarantee that they may not be called unto the greatest suffering of blood on account of their allegiance towards God.

2. The Discipline of God (12:5-11)

"..My son, despise not thou the chastening of the Lord," (vs. 5) But he enters here on the doctrine, that it is useful and needful for us to be disciplined by the cross; and he refers to the testimony of Solomon, which includes two parts; the first is, that we are not to reject the Lord's correction; and in the second the reason is given, because the Lord loves those whom he chastises. "Correction" is the best word for [παιδεία], as it stands for and not "chastening" or chastisement. "Despise" in Hebrew is to regard a thing as insignificant or with disrespect, and so in Greek it means to regard a thing as little; the meaning is, not stoical; and then the meaning of the next clause is, be not depending. "Fret not," or "be not faint" or despairing, "when reproved" or "chastised."The word "Discipline" is used both as a noun and as a verb. It denotes the training of a child. The word signifies

whatever teachers and parents do to train, correct and educate children for their development and maturity.

"For whom the Lord loveth he chasteneth,"(vs. 6) The emphasis of this passage is on the Heavenly Father's use of discipline in the lives of His children that He loves.Another value of divine discipline is that it prepares us to reign with Christ. (cf. 2:10) God's "discipline" assures us that we are His "sons." All believers are "partakers" (cf. 1:9; 3:1, 14; 6:4) of discipline. The "illegitimate children" in view seem to be genuine children of God but not approved sons. (Romans 8:14-17) There is a difference between children and sons. Ishmael is an Old Testament example of an illegitimate child. He was the true child of Abraham. Yet because he was "illegitimate" (i.e., the son of Hagar rather than Sarah, Abraham's wife), he did not receive the inheritance that Isaac, the legitimate child, did (cf. Gen. 17:19-21; 21:12-14). Ishmael received some blessings because he was Abraham's son, but he did not receive the full inheritance because he was an illegitimate child.

3. The need for Greater Strength (12:12-13)

"Wherefore lift up the hands which hang down, and the feeble knee," (v. 12) This word of exhortation, as well as the others, reveals that the original readers were spiritually weak. The author not only exhorts us to bear

afflictions with courage, but he also reminds us that there is no reason for us to be supine and sluggish in performing our duties. Many would be willing to acknowledge their faith, but as they fear persecution, hands and feet are wanting to that pious feeling of the mind. The author urged them to build up their strength (cf. Isa. 35:3), so they could work effectively and walk without stumbling (cf. Prov. 4:25-27).

The Greek word [ektrepo], translated *"be put out of joint"* (v. 13), has the technical medical sense of a foot turning and becoming dislocated. We need to strengthen those who suffer and help make the way easier for them, so that they will not fall away. We need to bear one another's burdens. (Galatians 6:2) *"And make straight paths for your feet,"* As then we seek tortuous courses, when entangled by sinful fear; so on the other hand everyone who has prepared himself to endure evils, goes on in a straight way whenever the Lord calls him. In short, he prescribes to us this rule for our conduct, which we are to guide our steps according to God's will, so that no fear or the allurements of the world, or any other things, may draw us away from it. Furthermore, it is a suitable way of speaking, for it is a worse thing to go astray than to halt. These that begin to halt do not immediately turn from the right way, but by degrees depart from it more and more, until having been led into a diverse path so they remain entangled in the midst of Satan's web. Consequently, the author warns us to strive for the removal of this halting in due time; for if we give way to it, it will at length turn us far away from God.

4. Follow peace and holiness (12:14, 15)

"Follow peace with all men, and holiness," (v. 14) The two exhortations, to follow peace with all men, and that holiness without which no one can see the Lord, consist of the whole Christian lifestyle. These two refer to our relation with God and with others. Man's nature makes him capable to shun peace; seek their own ways and interests, and care not to accommodate themselves to the ways of others.We need to live peaceably "with all people," as much as we can because peaceful interpersonal relations promote godliness (James 3:18). And this cannot be done unless we forget many offenses and exercise mutual forbearance. [29] In view of the fact

---

[29]It has been justly observed that διώκω is to follow or pursue one fleeing away from us. It means not only to seek peace but strive to maintain it. Psalm 34, we have pursuing after seeking, "Seek peace and pursue it," i.e., strive earnestly to secure and retain it. Romans 12:18, is an explanation. But this strenuous effort as to peace is to be extended to holiness; not chastity, as Chrysostom and some other fathers have imagined, but holiness in its widest sense, purity of heart and life, universal holiness. The word ἁγιασμὸς is indeed taken in a limited sense, and rendered "sanctification" 1 Thessalonians 4:3, and it may be so rendered here as it is in those places where it evidently means holiness universally, 1 Corinthians 1:30;2 Thessalonians 2:13,1 Peter 1:2. The article is put before it in

that we will one day see the Lord, and since no sin can abide in His presence (1 John 3:2), we must also pursue holiness in our lives now. A better translation than "sanctification" here is "holiness."In Greek [hagiasmos]; cf. [hagiatetos] in v. 10, and [hagiasomenoi] (10:10)

"Looking diligently lest any man fail of the grace of God ;"(v. 15) depressingly, the writer warned against neglecting *God's grace* which enables us to persevere (cf. 3:12), although here it is almost the same with the Christian faith. This neglect would result in unfaithfulness spreading as a poison of bitterness among God's people (cf. Deut. 29:17-18), or may be a source from which bitter error enters into the lives of other people, thus causing trouble. This can result in many other people being defiled, also going into error (1 Corinthians 5; 15:33; Matthew 18:6, 7; Joshua 7:25, 26).The author urges us to be diligent to watch out for evil influence. And that we must be constantly on guard. When Stubbornness grows, it produces the deadly fruit of apostasy, which is the same to excluding oneself from the grace of God.

---

order to show its connection with what follows, "and the (or that) holiness, without which no one shall see the Lord."

5. Lack of respect for God's blessings (12:16, 17)

"Lest there be any fornicator, or profane person, as Esau," (v. 16) As the author exhorted them to follow holiness (verses 14), he then warns them against defilements from "fornicators," "or a profane person;" for it is the term that is strictly contrary to holiness."Esau" is an example of someone who apostatized; he despised his inheritance ("birthright"; or "blessing"), and forfeited ("sold") it to satisfy his pressing desires. Esau could not regain his inheritance afterwards when he was in need of it. His incapacity to repent was not a matter of forgiveness, but of consequences. David is another example of a person who had to bear the consequences of his sins, even though God forgave him for those sins.

He warned against two things in verse 16: "immorality" Greek [pornos] and being "godless [bebelos] like Esau." The Old Testament makes no mention of Esau's immorality, so possibly he understood this term metaphorically in the sense of "apostate." On the other hand, Esau married two foreign wives, so in this sense he was an immoral fornicator (Gen.26:34-35; 27:46). Esau was "godless" in that he relinquished his covenant rights for the sake of abrupt enjoyment when he sold his birthright with food. Some translators rendered the Greek word [bebelos] "profane," which means "before (outside) the temple." "Esau's eagerness to give up all that was his as the firstborn son reflected contempt for the covenant by which his rights were justified. By descriptive analogy, he is representative of apostate the Hebrew Christians that were ready to turn their backs on God and the divine promises, in reckless disregard of the covenant blessings secured by the sacrificial death of Jesus.

"In Jewish history, the birthright belonged to the firstborn son in a family merely by right of birth and involved three things: ruler of the household under and for the father; priest of the family and the reception of a double portion of all the father's goods. Although a firstborn son did nothing whatsoever to come into possession of the birthright, he could conduct his life in such a manner so as to forfeit the birthright. He could not forfeit his position as firstborn in the family, but he could forfeit the rights of the firstborn.

6. A Contrast between Two Mountains (12:18-24)

The author proceeded to repeat the superiority of the New Covenant by comparing it with the Old Covenant, using the figure of two mountains: Sinai and Zion. These verses describe the giving of the Old Covenant at Mt.Sinai (cf. 2:2-4; Exod. 19:9-23; Deut. 4:11; 9:8-19). The Author made Sinai and Zion metaphors (symbols of the two covenants) to show the difference in quality between people's relationship to God under the Old and

New Covenants (cf. Gal.4:24-26). The stress in this comparison is on the holiness of God, and the fearful consequences of incurring His displeasure (Matt. 24:30-31; 1 Cor. 15:52; 1 Thess. 4:16). God was far from the Israelites, and even Moses was "full of fear and trembling."

The giving of the New Covenant and the things associated with that covenant, are more exciting as they encompass the heavenly realities. (12:22-24) These realities comprise the "heavenly city (Jerusalem)" (cf. Ps. 9:11; 76:2) and heavenly beings (i.e., "angels" and believers "spirits of the righteous made perfect." Everything about this vision encourages us to come boldly into God's presence. (cf. 4:16)

"First, the Mosaic covenant is a covenant of the senses because Mount Sinai was unapproachable yet perceivable by the senses. Second, the new covenant's Mount Zion is superior because it is unperceivable by the five senses while being approachable."

The phrase *"the general assembly and church of the firstborn"* the Greek construction suggests one group probably refers to; All those believers who had died, but will receive their full inheritance because of following the Lord. Another view is that it refers to all the saints on earth and in heaven. Others believe that only believers in the church are in view. Still other interpreters believe all Christians on earth are in view. Others believe all Christians already in heaven are.

Some believe that it refers to the angels just mentioned. And some believe that the "assembly" is the angels, and the "church" is the saints.

"To come to the 'church of the firstborn' means to be called to the privilege of being a firstborn son. All Christians are called to be part of that assembly and by birth have a right to be there. The "firstborn" was the son who received the greatest amount of inheritance and honour. The "church of the firstborn" is evidently another reference to Christ's companions (1:9; 3:12) who are partakers of His glory (3:14; 6:4; 12:8), namely, those who faithfully persevere in their faith. Their names are on a heavenly roll as those who died cleaving to the Lord (Isa. 4:3; Dan. 12:1; Luke 10:20; Phil. 4:3;Rev. 3:5; 13:8; 20:12).

Another view is that this refers to all Christians."The spirits of righteous men made perfect" evidently refers to all the glorified redeemed—faithful and unfaithful— whom Christ's sacrifice perfects eventually. (Glorifies; cf. 10:10, 14; 11:40) Some view these "spirits" as Old Testament believers.

Jesus' blood is "better" than Abel's, because Jesus' blood did not cry out for justice, retribution, and revenge as Abel's did (cf. 11:4; Gen. 4:10). It satisfied God's demands and secured God's acceptance of New Covenant believers (cf. 9:12, 26; 10:10, 14, and 19). It "speaks better," because it cries out to God for mercy and pardon on behalf of those for whom Jesus shed it.

Their "blood" is a metonymy for their "death." Both deaths were violent and involved the shedding of blood."It must be acknowledged that the reference to Abel in v. 24b is unexpected, because it does not belong to the developed comparison between Sinai and Zion. Therefore, it could have been recommended by the reference in v 23b to the presence of [pneumasi Dikaion] which means "the spirits of righteous people," in the heavenly city, since the author had specified in11:4 that Abel was attested by God as [dikaios], "righteous." It may also have been the author's intent to evoke the whole history of redemption, from the righteous Abel to the redemptive sacrifice of Jesus, mediator of the new covenant ..."These comparisons (vv. 18-21 and 22-24) should motivate us to remain faithful, and thereby realize the superior blessings of the New Covenant.

7. The consequences of apostasy (12:25-29)

Again we are warned not to refuse God's message or allow ourselves to be led away from this gospel back to that Old Covenant. *"See that ye refuse not him that speaketh."* (vs.25) is a negative way of saying *"Hear him."* The one "speaking" probably refers to God (cf. 1:1-2).He uses the same verb as before, when he said that the people entreated that God should not speak to them; but he means as I think, another thing, even that we ought not to reject the word intended for us. *"Him that spake on earth"*possibly refers to God when He spoke from Mt. Sinai. The contrast is not primarily between the persons who spoke, but between the places from which God spoke (vs. 26). Another view is that the contrast is between a human oracle of God (Moses) and the divine Voice (Christ). This contrast would have been remarkable mainly to the Hebrew Christians. *"Whose voice then shook the earth,"* however, God shook the earth when he gave his Law, yet he shows that he now speaks more gloriously, for he shakes both earth and heaven.That shaking will lead to the creation of new heavens and a new earth that will "remain" (Ps. 95:9-11; Hag. 2:6; Rev. 21:1). The "shaking" is a metaphor for the judgment of God executed in history, as in the case of the fall of Babylon announced in Isa 13:1-22.Now he quotes Prophet Haggai, though he gives not the words literally; but as the Prophet foretells a future shaking of the earth and the heaven. He explains to us that the voice of the Gospel not only thunders through the earth, but also penetrates above the heavens. *"I will shake all nations; and come shall the desire of all nations, and I will fill this house with glory."* It is however certain that neither all nations have been gathered into one body, except under the banner of Christ. The Prophet then no doubt refers to the time of Christ.

"For our God is a consuming fire," (vs. 28) since he had already set before us the grace of God, consequently he now makes known his sternness; and he seems to have borrowed this sentence from the Deuteronomy chapter 4.

Hence we observe that God omits nothing by which he may draw us to himself; he begins indeed with love and kindness, so that we may follow him the more willingly; but when by appealing he effects but little, he terrifies us.As a consuming fire, God purifies all that is undeserving and undesirable in those who serve Him and all that is unfit to abide in His presence.

Hebrews 13

D. Specific requirements of faithfulness (chapter 13)

1. Brotherly love, Hospitality, and Care for Prisoners (13:1-3)

"Let brotherly love." (vs. 1) This term refers to the special affection, appreciation, and attraction that Christians feel toward one another for being members of the same spiritual family. "The Hebrew Christians to whom this letter is addressed are flagging; it seems, not only in their zeal for the race on which they have set out (12:1, 12) but also in the ardor of their love for each other."[30] It is closely associated with our fellowship, communion, and mutual sharing. Brethren that have love for one another usually appreciate the good qualities that they see in one another without excusing sin. (1 Corinthians 12:12-27) They actually enjoy associating

---

[30]P. E. Hughes, A Commentary ..., p. 562.

together particularly in worshiping and serving the
LORD God (Hebrews 13:1, 2; Romans 12:10, 13). They
also care for one another and earnestly want to help one
another. (Romans 12:10, 13; 1 Corinthians 12:12-27;
Acts 2:42ff; 4:32ff) Their wish is to be united together in
serving the LORD. (Romans 15:5; 1 Corinthians 12:12-
27)
Brethren should be eager to share this love with all who
are brethren in Christ regardless of race, nationality,
background, etc. (John 15:12-17; Romans 8:16,17; 12:10
; 2 Corinthians 6:17,18; Galatians 3:28; Ephesians
4:2,31-5:2; 1:15; Colossians 1:9-11; Colossians 1:4,5;
Philippians 2:2,3; 2 Thessalonians 1:3;Philemon 1:5;
James 2:1-6,8,9;1 Peter 1:22; 2:17; 3:8,9; 4:8; 2Peter
1:1; Jude 3; 1 Thessalonians 3:6,12; 4:9,10; Hebrews
13:1; 1 John 1:6,7; 2:7-11. The word [philadelphos] in
Greek for "brethren" is mostly used in 1 John 3:10-18,
23; 4:8-5:3and John 13:34, 35. "Brotherly kindness" or
"the love of brothers (or sisters), brotherly love in the
N.T. is the love which Christians cherish for each other
as 'brethren'..." – Thayer.
"Be not forgetful to entertain strangers," (vs.2)
Abraham "entertained angels" when he showed them
hospitality (Gen. 18:1-3). Some in this way have even
entertained angels, as did Abraham and later Lot
(Genesis 18:3ff; 19:2ff). Note, however, that they did not
know they were so doing ("unconsciously") and neither
would we. But if we will be hospitable in general, when

the time might come, we would do as we should for them. Similarly, other people that entertained Angels were Lot (Gen. 19:1-3), Gideon (Judg. 6), and Manoah (Judg. 13). The word "Hospitality" Gk. [Philoxenia] literally means love of strangers. It involves an interest and concern for helping even people we don't know well. This may include helping Christians who are suffering from inflictions, Christians who are travelling such as preachers, helping new converts, and people who are new in the community, etc. The New Testament doctrine shows that all Christians should learn to practice hospitality to the extent of their ability. The emphasis in hospitality is in helping the needy, not just doing what people want done or what we enjoy for our own gratification such as having parties with others. It also emphasizes using one's home to meet the needs of other people. (Genesis 18:1-8; 19:1-3;2 Kings 4:8-11;Matthew 25:34-36,40; Luke 14:12-14; Acts 16:15; Romans 12:13; 1 Timothy 3:2; 5:9,10; 1 Peter 4:9; 3 John 5ff).

"Remember them that are in bonds, or, *Be mindful of the bound,"*(Vs.3) Further, he reminds them to be concerned for those in prison, putting yourself in their place as though you too were imprisoned (Matthew 25:36; Colossians 4:18; 2 Timothy 1:16). It appears the reference here may be to people who were imprisoned for the sake of their faithfulness to God (Hebrews 10:33ff; 11:36), for how could one identify as if imprisoned with people who are punished for crimes

they really committed? And remember people who are
suffering ill-treatment and wrongfully harmed by others.
We too are in the body, so we are subject to suffering,
and often do suffer. We should be able to sympathize
with those others who also suffering.

2. Marriage Life is to be honourable (13:4)

"Marriage is honorable in all," (vs.4) Marriage was
instituted by God (Genesis 2:18-24) and so is an
honorable relationship (1 Corinthians 7:38; Proverbs
18:22). The sexual union was equally fashioned by God
from the beginning and is essential to human procreation
(Genesis 1:26ff). All what God created was "very good,"
so this includes marriage and sexual relations within
marriage (Genesis 1:31; 1 Corinthians 7:2ff). Let this
then be the main point, that fornication will not be
unpunished, for God will take vengeance on it. And
doubtless as God has blessed the union of man and wife,
instituted by himself, it follows that every other union
different from this is by him condemned and accursed.
He therefore denounces punishment not only on
adulterers, but also on fornicators; for both depart from
the holy institution of God; they violate and undermine it
by a promiscuous intercourse, since there is but one
legitimate union, sanctioned by the authority and
approval of God. But as promiscuous and vagrant lusts
cannot be reserved without the remedy of marriage, he
therefore commends it by calling it "honorable."

3. Contentment and Divine provision (13:5, 6)

"Let your conversation be without covetousness," (vs.5)
Greediness has lured many believers away from a life of
trustworthy discipleship, as has sexual temptation. We
need to cultivate a spirit of contentment so that we do
not apostatize. Contentment really has nothing to do with
how much money we have, though the world generally
thinks it does. The LORD has promised never to
abandon ("desert" or "forsake") us (Matt. 28:20). "In
these circumstances, the Christian response is not to
grasp all the more eagerly at material wealth, but to rely
quietly on God's provision, even in the face of human
opposition."[31]"We may assume that love of money was
another temptation to which the recipients of this letter
were showing signs of giving in."[32]Apparently, these
Hebrews were losing some of their faith and trust in God
that had enabled them to endure the loss of possessions
and suffering persecution – 10:34. We are so wrapped up
in our desire for material things that we are hindered in
all aspects of true spirituality. We will involve ourselves
in all kinds of material pursuits to the neglect of God's
will for us. Contentment does not mean that we are
pleased with our difficult circumstances (2 Corinthians

[31]Ellingworth, p. 698.
[32]P. E. Hughes, A Commentary …, p. 567.

12:7-10). Perhaps since God has given the ability to make money to many Jewish people, this was a particularly appropriate word of caution for the original readers.

While he seeks to correct covetousness, he rightly and wisely bids us at the same time to be content with our present things; for it is the true contempt of money. When we are content with what the Lord has given us, whether it much or little; for certainly it rarely happens that anything satisfies a covetous man; but on the contrary they who are not content with a moderate portion, always seek more even when they enjoy the greatest affluence. It was a doctrine which Paul had declared, that he had learned, so as to know how to abound and how to suffer need. Then, he who has set limits to his desire so as to assent resignedly in his lot, has expelled from his heart the love of money.

4. Religious Duties (13:7-19)

The example of our spiritual leaders is one that we should follow or "imitate" (cf. 12:1; 13:17, 24). They, like the heroes of faith in chapter 11, set a good pattern. They may have been the founders of the church to which this letter went. People tend to forget or to idolize their former leaders, but we should "remember" them, "considering" their godly teachings and examples (1 Thess. 5:12-13).

"Jesus Christ the same," (vs. 8) Jesus Christ is the content of the message that the leaders had preached to these hearers that are mentioned in verse 7. That message is what this author had urged his readers not to abandon. The leaders had preached the Word of God to these readers, and that preaching culminated in Jesus Christ.Nevertheless, the only way by which we can persevere in the right faith is to hold to the foundation, and not in the smallest degree to depart from it; for he who holds not to Christ knows nothing but mere vanity, though he may comprehend heaven and earth; for in Christ are included all the treasures of celestial wisdom. "Jesus is not the object of faith [in this verse or in Hebrews, according to this author], but the supreme model of it."[33]*The same,* he says, *yesterday, and today, and forever.* By which words he intimates that Christ, who was then made known in the world, had reigned from the beginning of the world, and that it is not possible to advance farther when we come to him. *Yesterday* then comprehends the whole time of the Old Testament; and that no one might anticipate a sudden change after a short time, as the dissemination of the Gospel was then but recent, he declares that Christ had been lately revealed for this very end, that the knowledge of him might continue the same forever."Yesterday" the original leaders preached Jesus Christ, even as the author

---

[33]G. W. MacRae, "Heavenly Temple and Eschatology in the Letter to the Hebrews," Semeia12 (1978):194.

does now. The present time can tolerate no other approach to the grace of God (2:9). 'Forever' recalls the quality of the redemption secured by Jesus Christ (5:9; 9:12,14-15; 13:20) and of the priesthood of Christ(7:24-25): it is "eternal."

"Divers and strange doctrines,"(vs. 9) The author concludes that we ought not to fluctuate, given that the truth of Christ, in which we must stand firm, remains fixed and unchangeable. We should reject wrong teachings that deviate from apostolic doctrine. This, too, is a strong safeguard against apostasy. The terms "divers and strange" describe a variety of heretical positions. Instead of accepting these ideas, we should receive strength by taking in God's 'grace' that comes through His Word (4:12-13; 1 Pet. 2:2). The doctrines which lead us away from Christ are *divers* or various because there is no other truth than the knowledge of Christ. The author also calls them strange or foreign, because whatever is apart from Christ is not regarded by God as his own; and we are hereby also reminded how we are to proceed, if we would make a due proficiency in the Scripture. The author farther intimates that the Church of God will always have to contend with strange doctrines and that there is no other means of guarding against them but by being fortified with the pure knowledge of Christ. [34]

---

34 "Doctrines" were said to be "various" because of their number; there were then as now many false doctrines; and "strange" because they were new or foreign to the truth, not consistent with the faith,

Evidently one of the "strange" teachings, widespread when this letter originated, was that eating certain foods, or abstinence from certain foods, resulted in greater godliness (cf. Col. 2:16;1 Tim. 4:1-5). This was actually what Judaism taught. It taught that eating food "strengthened the heart," in the sense that when the Jews ate, they also gave thanks to God, and therefore brought Him into their experience (cf. Ps.104:14-15).

"For it is a good thing," (vs. 9) These Hebrews were superstitious as to distinctions in meats; and hence arose many disputes and discords. This was one of the strange doctrines which proceeded from their ignorance of Christ. Having then previously grounded our faith on Christ, he now says that the observance of meats does not conduce to our salvation and true holiness. As he sets *grace* in opposition to *meats*, I doubt not but that by grace he means the spiritual worship of God and spiritual transformation. In saying *"that the heart may be established,"* (vs. 9) he alludes to the word, *"carried about,"* as though he had said, It is the spiritual grace of God, and not the observance of meats, that will really establish us.

"Which have not profited them that have been occupied therein," (vs. 9) It is uncertain to whom he refers to here; for the fathers who lived under the Law had no doubt a useful training, and a part of it was the distinction as to

---

but derived from abroad as it were, borrowed from traditions, ceremonies, or other foreign sources. Stuart gives another meaning

meats. It seems then that this is to be understood rather of the superstitious, which after the Gospel had been revealed, still perversely adhered to the old covenant ceremonies. At the same time were we prudently to explain the words as applied to the fathers, there would be no inconsistency; it was indeed profitable for them to undergo the yoke laid on them by the Lord, and to continue obediently under the common discipline of the godly and of the whole Church. However, the author means that abstinence from meats was in itself of no avail and it is to be regarded as nothing, except as an elementary instruction at the time when God's people were like children as to their external discipline. To be "occupied *in meats*" is to be taken as having a regard to them, so as to even make a distinction between clean and unclean. But what he says of meats may be extended to the other rites of the Law.

"We have an altar," (vs. 10) This is a lovely adaptation of an old rite under the Law, to the present state of the Church. "Christians had none of the visible apparatus which in those days was habitually associated with religion and worship—no sacred buildings, no altars, no sacrificing priests. Their pagan neighbors thought they had no God, and called them atheists; their Jewish neighbors too might criticize them for having no visible means of spiritual support.[35] Likewise, the Old

---

[35]Bruce, The Epistle ..., p. 400.

Testament had its regulations regarding meats, etc. Meats were offered as animal sacrifices and then people ate them (verse 11; Leviticus 6:26-30; 7:11-15). Believers under the Old Covenant ate part of what they offered to God as a peace offering (Lev. 7:15-18). However, believers under the New Covenant feed spiritually on Jesus Christ, who is our Peace Offering. Those still under the Old Covenant ("who serve the tabernacle") had "no right" to partake of Him for spiritual sustenance and fellowship with God, since their confidence (faith) was still in the Old Covenant. You cannot partake of both the Old Testament and the New Testament (Galatians 5:3,4). There were several restrictions regarding eating of clean and unclean meats but did not save anyone. (Colossians 2:14-17). Therefore, those regulations on foods are not essential in any way to our salvation.

Furthermore, Old Testament priests offered sacrifices on the altar, and then people ate those sacrifices. Jesus, our high priest had offered himself for us once and for all (9:11ff) and he became our altar. It was not literal but symbolized by the Old Testament altar, where the animals were slain. Those who want to continue under the Old Testament with its altar will receive none of the benefit of this sacrifice. If you choose the Old, you cannot partake of the New, and that means you have no sacrifice that can remove sins. You are without Christ and without hope. You have returned to a system that

Jesus died to remove. This is what the Hebrews must remember regarding going back to the Old Testament.

5. Jesus suffered outside the camp (13:11-13)

"For the bodies of those beasts, whose blood is brought into the sanctuary by the high priest for sin" (vs. 11)In the Old Covenant, some animal sacrifices were eaten by the people (verses 9, 10 above). But the animals that were sacrificed for the sins of the people had to be burned outside the camp of the people (Exodus 29:14; Leviticus 4:12, 21; 6:30; 9:11; 16:27; Numbers 19:3, 7). This seems to symbolize the fact that the animal was not fit to be among God's people because it bore their sins, it had to be rejected or alienated from the people. Here the author compared Jesus to the "sin offering" that the Jewish high priest offered on the Day of Atonement (cf. Lev. 16:27)."... in Hebrews the expression 'high priest 'customarily signals that the field of reference is the annual atonement ritual (cf. 5:3; 7:27; 8:1-3;9:7, 11, 12, 24-26)."[36]Jesus' death "outside" Jerusalem (the gate) fulfilled the Day of Atonement ritual *"Wherefore Jesus also"*(v. 12), in that the high priest "burned" the remains of the two sacrificial animals "outside" the grounds of the wilderness "camp" (v. 11). This also fulfilled the ritual of that day, in that Jesus' execution "outside" the

[36]Lane, Hebrews 9—13, p. 540.

city (gate) involved the shame of exclusion from the sacred precincts. It therefore symbolized His rejection by the Jewish authorities.

"Let us go forth therefore," (vs. 13) The author invites us to leave the tabernacle and to follow Christ, he reminds us that a far different thing is required of us from the work of serving God in the shade under the glorious splendor of the temple. We must go after him through exiles, flights, reproaches, and all kinds of afflictions. This warfare, in which we must strive even unto blood, he sets in opposition to those shadowy practices of which alone the teachers of ceremonies boasted.Christians bear Jesus' "reproach" when they identify with Him. Jesus suffered reproach (insults, shame, and rejection), and so do we, but only when we identify with His name and person. The Christian Hebrews needed to cut their emotional and religious ties to Judaism. The exhortation let us go forth therefore, *unto him* means that no longer must the readers look for salvation in the old forms of Judaism; they must come outside of it to Jesus who cannot be found in Judaism. The exhortation to leave the camp [i.e., official Judaism] and to identify fully with Jesus introduces a unique understanding of discipleship. Jesus' action in going 'outside the camp' (v 12) set a standard for others to follow. It entails the costly commitment to follow him resolutely, despite suffering. In the context of the

allusion to Golgotha in v 12, this order to discipleship implies following Jesus on the way to the cross.

6. The Heavenly Jerusalem (13:14)

"For here we have no continuing city" (vs. 14) He again extends the going forth which he had mentioned that we are strangers in this world. We should consider that we have no fixed residence but in heaven and the "city" we seek is the heavenly Jerusalem. Our present habitation on earth is only temporary (cf. 11:26). The author teaches us here, that we have no definite shade on earth, for heaven is our inheritance; and when more and more tried, let us ever prepare ourselves for our last end; for they who enjoy a very quiet life commonly imagine that they have a rest in this world: it is hence profitable for us, who are prone to this kind of sloth, to be often tossed here and there, that we who are too much inclined to look on things below, may learn to turn our eyes up to heaven.

7. The sacrifices of praise to God and service to others (13:15, 16)

"By him, therefore, let us offer the sacrifice of praise to God," (vs. 15) The author had taught us that as Christ had suffered without the gate, we are also called thither, and that hence the tabernacle must be forsaken by those who would follow him. He is now teaching us the

genuine way of worshipping God under the New Testament. He reminds us that God cannot be really invoked by us and his name glorified, except through Christ the mediator; for it is he alone who sanctifies our lips, which otherwise are unclean, to sing the praises of God; and it is he who opens a way for our prayers, who in short performs the office of a priest, presenting himself before God in our name.

"But to do good," (vs. 16) For though he can derive no benefit from us, yet he regards prayer a sacrifice, and so much as the chief sacrifice, that it alone can supply the place of all the rest; and then, whatever benefits we confer on men he considers as done to himself, and honors them with the name of sacrifices. Although the ancient sacrifices have been abolished, there is one which can never grow old-the *sacrifice of praise.* This incense must ever rise from the heart-altar. Subsequently it appears that the fundamentals of the Law are now not only unessential, but do harm, as they draw us away from the right way of sacrificing. The meaning is that if we wish to sacrifice to God, we must call on him and accept his goodness by thanksgiving, and that we must do good to our brethren. These are the true sacrifices which Christians ought to offer; and as to other sacrifices, there is neither time nor place for them.

"For with such sacrifices God is well pleased,"(vs. 16) There is to be understood here an implied contrast, —

that he no longer requires those ancient sacrifices which he had enjoined until the abrogation of the Law. But with this doctrine is connected an exhortation which ought powerfully to stimulate us to exercise kindness towards our neighbors; for it is not a common honor that God should regard the benefits we confer on men as sacrifices offered to Himself, and that he so adorns our works, which are nothing worth, as to pronounce them holy and sacred things, acceptable to Him. When, therefore, love does not prevail among us, we not only rob men of their right, but God himself, who has by a solemn sentence dedicated to himself what he has commanded to be done to men."The word *communicate* has a wider meaning than *to do good,* for it embraces all the duties by which men can mutually assist one another; and it is a true mark or proof of love, when they who are

---

[37] The words may be thus rendered, "And forget not benevolence (or, literally, well-doing) and liberality." The δὲ here should be rendered "and," for this is enjoined in addition to what is stated in the previous verse. The word εὐποιΐα means kindness, benevolence, beneficence, the doing of good generally; but κοινωνία refers to the distribution of what is needful for the poor. See Romans 15:26, 2 Corinthians 9:13. So that Calvin in this instance has reserved their specific meaning. Stuart's version is "Forget not kindness also and liberality;" and he explains the clause thus, "Beneficence or kindness toward the suffering and liberality toward the needy."

united together by the Spirit of God communicate to one another.[37]

8. Obedience to the rulers and those that watch for our souls (13:17)

"Obey them, for they watch for your souls", (vs. 17) This is referring to"leaders" particularly church elders. These shepherds *"watch over your souls,"* and will one day give account to God for their stewardship over the souls of many.His meaning is, that the heavier the burden they bear, the more honor they deserve; for the more labor anyone undertakes for our sake, and the more difficulty and danger he incurs for us, the greater are our obligations to him. And such is the office of bishops, that it involves the greatest labor and the greatest danger; if, then, we wish to be grateful, we can hardly render to them that which is due; and especially, as they are to give an account of us to God, it would be disgraceful for us to make no account of them. Thus, we ought to make their work in this life easier for them through obedience and submissive to them. He also bids us to be teachable and ready to obey, that what pastors do in effect of what their office demands, they may also eagerly and *gladly* do; for, if they have their minds filled with sorrow or exhaustion, though they may be sincere and faithful, they will yet become disheartened and careless. For this reason the author declares, that it would be *unprofitable*

to the people to cause sorrow and mourning to their pastors by their ingratitude.

The presence of this exhortation at this point in the letter may imply that the racially Jewish element in the church tended to be unsubmissive. He commands first obedience and then honor to be rendered to them. [38] These things are necessarily required so that the people might have confidence in their pastors, and also reverence for them. He is speaking only of those who faithfully performed their office. And this also is what the author clearly sets forth when he says, that they *watched* for their souls, — a duty which is not performed but by those who are faithful rulers, and are really what they are called.

9. Final Prayer and salutations (13:18-25)

[38] Grotius renders the second verb, ὑπείκετε, "concede" to them, that is, the honor due to their office; Beza, "be compliant," (obsecundate;) and the directions of your guides and submit to their admonitions." Doddridge gives the sentiment of Calvin, "Submit yourselves to them with becoming respect." The words may be rendered, "Obey your rulers and be submissive;" that is cultivate an obedient, compliant and submissive spirit. He speaks first of what they were to do — to render obedience and then of the spirit with which that obedience was to be rendered; it was not merely to be an outward act, but proceeding from a submissive mind. Schleusner's explanation is similar, "Obey your rulers and promptly (or willingly) obey them."

"Pray for us: For we trust," (vs. 18) After having applauded himself to their prayers so that he motivates them to pray even more, he now declares that he had a *good conscience. H*e mentions the integrity of his own conscience, that is, that he might move them more effectually to feel an interest for himself. *"But I beseech you,"* (vs.19) *Again* he brings another argument, — that the prayers they would make for him, would be profitable to them all as well as to himself. The author of this letter was either overwhelmed with predicament or apprehended by the fear of persecution, so as not to be able to come to those to whom he was writing. *"Now the God of peace,"* (vs. 20) He ends his letter with prayer; and he asks God to *validate* or to perfect them in *"every good work"* (vs.21) because such is the meaning of [καταρτίσαι] We are by no means fit to do good until we are made or formed for the purpose by God, and that we shall not continue long in doing good unless he strengthens us. *"That brought again from the dead,"* (vs. 20) This phrase was included for the sake of confirmation. The author wants his hearers to look to Christ so that they may appropriately trust in God for help since Christ was raised from death for this end, that we might be renewed unto eternal life by the same power of God. The phrase *"Through the blood, "*(vs. 20) may well be rendered as *"In the blood"* for "in," is generally taken in the sense of *with*. This appears to me that the author means that Christ arose from the dead and that his

death was not yet abolished but that it retains its effectiveness forever, as though he had said, "God raised up his own son, but in such a way that the blood he shed once for all in his death is efficacious after his resurrection for the ratification of the everlasting covenant, and brings forth fruit the same as though it were flowing always." *"To do his will,"* (vs. 21) He now gives a description of good works by laying down God's *will* as the rule. He explains that no works are to be deemed good unless they are pleasurable to the will of God, as Apostle Paul also teaches us (Romans 12:2).It is therefore, the perfection of a good and holy life when we live in obedience to His *will* ."*working in you what is well pleasing in his sight,"* The author here had spoken of that *will* which is made known in the Law; he now shows worthless all what God has not commanded because He only values the decrees of his own *will* far more than all the inventions of the world.*"Through Jesus Christ,"* This phrase may be explained in two ways in which both interpretations seem suitable, — either "Working through Jesus Christ", or, "Well pleasing through Jesus Christ." For we know that the spirit of regeneration and also all graces are bestowed on us through Christ; and then it is certain that as nothing can proceed from us absolutely perfect, nothing can be acceptable to God without that pardon which we obtain through Christ. Thus, our works performed by the aroma of Christ's grace, release a sweet fragrance in God's presence or else they would have a rotten smell.

"And I beseech you," (vs. 22) The closing verses of Hebrews are an appendix to the body of this homiletical letter. The author added them because he felt pastoral concern for his addressees and because he wanted to include a few personal remarks. He again urged his readers to accept ("bear with") the "word of exhortation" contained in this letter instead of rejecting it. This is the Greek word [paraklasis] (exhortation) which means imploration, supplication, entreaty, admonition, encouragement, consolation, comfort, and solace."The definite expression 'the exhortation' is a synonymous designation for the sermon. It referred specifically to the exposition and application of the Scripture that had been read aloud to the assembled congregation. In a fourth century description of the liturgy for the consecration of a bishop the homily is designated Thayer, A Greek-English Lexicon of the New Testament [paraklasis], p. 483.logous [parakleseos] , 'words of exhortation'(Apost. Const.8.5). This appears to be a fixed expression for the sermon in early Christian circles..."

"Know ye that our brother," (vs. 23) *Since* the termination of the Greek verb [γινώσκετε], will admit of either renderings, we may read, "Ye know," or, "Know ye;" but I prefer the latter reading, though I do not reject

the other. [39] The author observably wrote this letter at the
time Timothy was living and after some imprisonment
that he had experienced. It is clear that the author and
Timothy were close associates in the Lord's work. This is
almost certainly a reference to the same "Timothy" who
was known as Paul's "son in the faith," referred to
elsewhere in the New Testament. This is the only Saint
that the author mentioned by name in the letter.

"Salute," (vs. 24) The author now sends this salutation,
more particularly to the rulers, as a mark of honor so that
he may reconcile them and kindly lead them to "agree to
his doctrine. And he adds, *"And all the saints"* (vs. 24)
to either mean the faithful from among the Gentiles, and
refers to them that both Jews and Gentiles might learn to
cultivate unity among themselves; or his aim was to
intimate that they who first received the letter, were to
communicate it to others. The word "leaders" refers to
local church leaders (vv. 7, 17). The letter probably went
to one house-church and evidence indicates that most
first-century churches had more than one leader (cf. Acts
14:23; 20:17; Titus 1:5; Phil. 1:1). It would be strange
for the author to send this letter to someone in a church
who was not a leader. The members of the several house
churches in particular houses needed to keep in touch
with one another. It was of vital importance that the
greetings of the writer be conveyed to *"all the*

39The Vulgate Beza and almost all expounders, render it as an
imperative, "Know ye."

saints." "They of Italy salute you," There are two possible views that may well explain this phrase. The first view refers to Christians who had left Italy rather than to believers currently living there (Acts18:2). If this is true, the author most likely wrote from somewhere other than Italy. The other view is that "those from Italy" refers to Christians living in Italy who joined the author in sending greetings. If the letter went originally to Christian Jews in Rome, the writer may have been writing from somewhere else in Italy.

"Grace be with you all," (vs. 25) However, author closed with a final benediction and prayer that God's "grace" would "be with" his readers, in the sense that they would receive strength from it (2:9; 4:16; 10:29; 12:15;13:9). This would happen as they persevered faithfully in the truth. The whole of this last chapter of the book of Hebrews is an admonition to worship God suitably according to the New Covenant.

BIBLIOGRAPHY

For a study of salvation in Hebrews, see Brenda B. Colijn, "'Let Us Approach': Soteriology in the Epistle to the Hebrews," Journal of the Evangelical Theological Society 39:4(December 1996):571-86.

Brown, Raymond, *The Message of Hebrews.* Ed. by John RW Stott. Leicester: Intervarsity Press, 1982.

Bruce, F. F. The Epistle to the Hebrews. New International Commentary on the New Testament series. Grand Rapids: Wm. B. Eerdmans Publishing Co., 1964.

_____. "The Kerygma of Hebrews." Interpretation 23:1 (January 1969):3-19.

Cross, Frank M. "The Tabernacle." Biblical Archaeologist 10:3 (September 1947):45-68.

Ellingworth, Paul. The Epistle to the Hebrews: A Commentary on the Greek Text . The New International Greek Testament Commentary series. Grand Rapids: Wm. B. Eerdmans Publishing Co.; and Carlisle, England: Paternoster Press, 1993.

Guthric, Doneld, *New Testament Theology.*Secunderabad: Intervarsity Press, 1981.

Guthrie, Donald. *Tyndale NT Commentaries Hebrews.* Leicester: InterVarsity Press, 1983.

Guthrie George, *Hebrews NIV application commentary*, ed. By Terry Muck, Michigan: Zondervan, 1998.

Horne, Thomas, *Introduction to the Critical Study and Knowledge of the Holy Scriptures*, 4 volumes; T. Cadwell, Strand, London, 1828 (public domain)

Hughes, R. Kent. Hebrews: An Anchor for the Soul . 2 vols. Wheaton: Crossway Books, 1993.

Hughes, Philip Edgcumbe. "The Blood of Jesus and His Heavenly Priesthood in Hebrews." Bibliotheca Sacra 130:518 (April-June 1973):99-109; 519 (July-September 1973):195-212; 520 (October-December 1973):305-14; 131:521 (January-March 1974):26-33.

_____. A Commentary on the Epistle to the Hebrews . Reprint ed. Grand Rapids: Wm. B. Eerdmans Publishing Co., 1983.

_____. "Hebrews 6:4-6 and the Peril of Apostasy." Westminster Theological Journal 35 (1973):137-55.

Josephus, Flavius. The Works of Flavius Josephus . Translated by William Whiston. London: T. Nelson and Sons, 1866; reprint ed. Peabody, Mass.: Hendrickson Publishers, 1988.

King, Daniel H., Sr., *The Book of Hebrews*; Guardian of Truth Foundation, Bowling Green, KY, 2008

Lane, William L. Hebrews 1-8 . Word Biblical Commentary series. Dallas: Word Books, 1991.

_____. Hebrews 9—13 . Word Biblical Commentary series. Dallas: Word Books, 1991.

MacRae, G. W. "Heavenly Temple and Eschatology in the Letter to the Hebrews." Semeia 12 (1978):179-99.

Mac Arthur, John. *The Mac Arthur NT Commentary:Hebrews.* Chicago: MBI, 1983.

Milligan, R., *Commentary on Hebrews*; Gospel Light Publishing Co., Delight, Arkansas

Moffatt, James. A Critical and Exegetical Commentary on the Epistle to the Hebrews. International Critical Commentary series. Reprint ed. Edinburgh: T. and T. Clark, 1963.

Morris, Leon. "Hebrews." In Hebrews-Revelation . Vol. 12 of the Expositor's Bible Commentary. 12 vols. Edited by Frank E. Gaebelein. Grand Rapids: Zondervan Publishing House, 1981.

Moseley, W.C., *Notes on the Book of Hebrews*; Cogdill Foundation, Marion, IN, 1971

Notes onHebrews2 0 2 0 E d i t i o n by Dr. Thomas L. Constable

Robertson, Archibald Thomas. Word Pictures in the New Testament . 6 vols. Nashville: Broadman Press, 1931.

Robinson, S. E. "The Apocraphal Story of Melchizedek." Journal for the Study of Judaism 18:1 (June 1987):26-39.

Selby, Gary S. "The Meaning and Function of Suneidesis in Hebrews 9 and 10." Restoration Quarterly 28:3 (Third Quarter 1985/86):145-54.

Thayer, Joseph Henry, *Greek-English Lexicon of the New Testament* (original material prepared by Grimm and Wilke, translated, revised, and enlarged by Thayer); Zondervan's Publishing House, Grand Rapids, MI (public domain)

Vine, W.E., *Vine's Expository Dictionary of New Testament Words*; MacDonald Publishing Co., McLean, VA

Welch, Robert C., *Living by Faith: Commentary on Hebrews*; Faith and Facts Press, Erlanger, KY, 1980

Other Sources

1. He calls them "holy brethren." Stuart takes holy as meaning "consecrated, devoted, i.e. to Christ, set apart as Christians." The people of Israel were called holy in the same sense, not because they were spiritually holy, but because they were set apart and adopted as God's people. The word saint, at the commencement of Paul's Epistles, means the same thing. (2)

2. It is better for "hope" here to be retained in its proper meaning; for in verse 12 the defect of it is traced to unbelief. Were the words "confidence" and "rejoicing" rendered adjectivally, the meaning would be more evident, — "If we hold firm our confident and joyful hope to the end." So we may render a similar form of expression in verse 13, "through deceitful sin," as "newness of life" in Romans 6:4, means "new life." The most common practice is to render the genitive in such instances as an adjective, but this is not always the case. Hope is "confident" or assured, while it rests on the word of God, and is "joyful" while it anticipates the glory and happiness of the heavenly kingdom. But Beza and Doddridge take words apart, "freedom of profession and boasting of hope," or according to Beza, "the hope of which we boast." Macknight renders them "the boldness and the glorifying of the hope." The secondary meaning of the word παρρησία is confidence, and of καύχημα, joy or rejoicing, and the most suitable here, as it comports better with holding fast, or firm. (3)

3. This passage, "Thou art my Son," etc., in this place, is only adduced to show that Christ was the Son of God: Christ did not honor or magnify or exalt himself, (for so δοξάζω means here,) but he who said to him, "Thou art my son," etc., did honor or exalt him. This is the meaning of the sentence. The verse may thus be rendered, — 5. So also Christ, himself he did not exalt to be a high priest, but he who had said to him, "My son art thou, I have this day begotten thee." It is the same as though he had said, "Christ did not make himself a high priest but God." And the reason why he speaks

of God as having said "My Son," etc., seems to be this, — to show that he who made him king (for the reference in Psalm 2 is to his appointment as a king) made him also a high priest. And this is confirmed by the next quotation from Psalm 110; for in the first verse he is spoken of as a king, and then in verse 4 his priesthood is mentioned.(4)

4. Stuart on this passage very justly observes, "If Jesus died as a common virtuous suffered, and merely as a martyr to the truth, without any vicarious suffering laid upon him, then is his death a most unaccountable event in respect to the manner of his behavior while suffering it; and it must be admitted that multitudes of humble.(6)

5. The word τελειωθείς, means here the same as in chapter 2:10. Stuart gives it the same meaning here as in the former passage, "Then when exalted to glory," etc.; but this does not comport with what follows, for it was not his exaltation to glory that qualified him to be "the author (or the causer or effecter) of eternal salvation," but his perfect or complete work in suffering, by his having completely and perfectly performed the work of atonement. And that his suffering in obedience to God's will, even his vicarious suffering, is meant here, appears also from the following reference to his being a priest after the order of Melchisedec. The meaning then seems to be, that Christ having fully completed his work as a priest, and that by suffering, became thereby the author of eternal salvation. (7)

6. Rather, "Yet even the first," etc. It is connected with the last verse of the preceding chapter; as though he had said, — "Though the covenant is become antiquated, yet it had many things divinely appointed connected with it." Μὲνοῦν mean "yet," or however. See Art. 8:4. Macknight has "Now verily;" and Stuart, "Moreover."(9)

7. Macknight makes this "entrance" to be death! As though the Apostle was speaking of what was future, while in verse 22, with which the contents of this verse and the following are connected, he says, "let us draw near;" that is, we who have this entrance, even "the new and living way." Possessing such a privilege, they were to

draw nigh. It is clearly an entrance and a way which believers now possess.(14)

8. This true, sincere, or upright heart, freed from vice and pollution, was symbolized by the washing at the end of the verse. Without washing the priests were not allowed to minister, and were threatened with death, Exodus 30:19-21; and when any of them touched an unclean thing, he was not allowed to eat of holy things until he washed himself, see 12:6 [sic]. Washing the body was a most important thing, as it symbolized the inward washing of the heart, which alone makes us true, or sincere, or faithful to God. We have here two things — a sincere heart, and assurance of faith: the last is then set forth by sprinkling, a word borrowed for Levitical rites; and the first by the washing of the body as under the law. (15)

9. Πονηρὸς means in Hebrew, the evil of sin wicked, and also the effect of sin, miserable It seems to be in the latter sense here; a miserable conscience is one oppressed with guilt. So Grotius and Stuart regard the meaning. It is the same as "consciousness of sin" in verse 2. What seems to be meant is an accusing or guilty conscience, laboring under the pressure of conscious sin. But Doddridge and Scott, like Calvin, combine the two ideas of guilt and pollution; though washing, afterwards mentioned, appears more appropriately to refer to the latter; and forgiveness is what is most commonly connected with the blood of Christ.(16)

10. The words literally are "In Isaac shall be called to thee a seed." But the Hebrew and the Greek ἐν, mean often by or through, or by the means of: and the Hebrew verb, to be called, as well as the Greek, may sometimes be rendered to be. Hence Macknight seems to have been right in his version of the clause, "By Isaac a seed shall be thee;" which is better than that of Stuart, "After Isaac shall thy seed be named," for this is less literal, and the meaning is not conveyed. (20)

11. The meaning given by Stuart and some others is very far fetched, though said to be natural, that "Abraham believed that God could raise Isaac from the dead, because he had, as it were, obtained him from the dead, i.e., he was born of those who were dead as to

these things." Hence the rendering given is "comparatively." Abraham had, as to his purpose, sacrificed him, so that he considered him as dead; and he received him back from the dead, not really, but in a way bearing a likeness to such a miracle. This sense is alone compatible with the former clause, which mentions Abraham's faith in God's power to raise his son from the dead; he believed that God was able to do this; and then it is added that Abraham had received back his son as though he had sacrificed him, and as though God had raised him from the dead. What actually took place bore a likeness to the way which he had anticipated. Costallio gives the meaning, "it was the same as though he had sacrificed him, and received him also in a manner he received him." (21)

12. Literally it is "when he became great," that is, in age or in years: he was, as it appears from Acts 7:23, about forty years of age. The word "great," both in Hebrew and Greek, has sometimes this meaning. "When arrived at mature age," by Stuart, is better than "when he was grown up," by Doddridge and Macknight. It is said that he refused, that is by his conduct. He acted in such a way as to show that he rejected the honor of being adopted son of Pharoah's daughter. The verb means to deny, to renounce, to disown. He renounced the privilege offered to him. Others are said to "deny the power" of godliness, that is by their works. 2 Timothy 3:5. (23)

13. And it has been adopted by many of the German divines, who seem in many instances to follow any vagary, Rabbinical or heathen, rather than the word of God. There is nothing in Scripture that countenances this notion. The word is never used in the sense of a hostess: and the ancient versions ever render the Hebrew word by πόρνη, a harlot. (26)

14. The history of Gideon we have in Judges 6:11, to the end of the 8th chapter: of Barak, in Judges 4:6, to the end of the 5th: of Samson, in Judges 13:24, to the end of the 16th: and of Jephthah, in Judges 11:1, to the end of the 12th chapter. Thus we see that the order of time in which they lived is not here observed, it being not necessary for the object of the author. Barak was before Gideon, Jephthah before Samson, and Samuel before David. (27)

15. The τύμπανον was, according to Schleusner, a machine on which the body was stretched; and then cudgels or rods, and whips were used. This appears from the account given in 2 Macc. 6: 19, 30. It is said that Eleasar, rather than transgress the Law, went of his own accord "to the torment" — ἐπὶ τὸτύμπανον, and in the 30th verse mention is made of stripes or strokes — πληγαῖς, and of being lashed or whipped — μαστιγούμενος. This was to be tympanized or tortured. (28)

16. It has been justly observed that διώκω is to follow or pursue one fleeing away from us. It means not only to seek peace but strive to maintain it. Psalm 34, we have pursuing after seeking, "Seek peace and pursue it," i.e., strive earnestly to secure and retain it. Romans 12:18, is an explanation. But this strenuous effort as to peace is to be extended to holiness; not chastity, as Chrysostom and some other fathers have imagined, but holiness in its widest sense, purity of heart and life, universal holiness. The word ἁγιασμὸς is indeed taken in a limited sense, and rendered "sanctification" 1 Thessalonians 4:3, and it may be so rendered here as it is in those places where it evidently means holiness universally, 1 Corinthians 1:30;2 Thessalonians 2:13,1 Peter 1:2. The article is put before it in order to show its connection with what follows, "and the (or that) holiness, without which no one shall see the Lord." (29)

17. Doctrines" were said to be "various" because of their number; there were then as now many false doctrines; and "strange" because they were new or foreign to the truth, not consistent with the faith, but derived from abroad as it were, borrowed from traditions, ceremonies, or other foreign sources. Stuart gives another meaningBruce, The Epistle …, p. 400.(34)

18. The words may be thus rendered, "And forget not benevolence (or, literally, well-doing) and liberality." The δὲ here should be rendered "and," for this is enjoined in addition to what is stated in the previous verse. The word εὐποιΐα means kindness, benevolence, beneficence, the doing of good generally; but κοινωνία refers to the distribution of what is needful for the poor. See Romans 15:26, 2 Corinthians 9:13. So that Calvin in this instance has reserved their specific meaning. Stuart's version is "Forget not kindness also and

liberality;" and he explains the clause thus, "Beneficence or kindness toward the suffering and liberality toward the needy."(37)

19. Grotius renders the second verb, ὑπείκετε, "concede" to them, that is, the honor due to their office; Beza, "be compliant," (obsecundate;) and the directions of your guides and submit to their admonitions." Doddridge gives the sentiment of Calvin, "Submit yourselves to them with becoming respect." The words may be rendered, "Obey your rulers and be submissive;" that is cultivate an obedient, compliant and submissive spirit. He speaks first of what they were to do — to render obedience and then of the spirit with which that obedience was to be rendered; it was not merely to be an outward act, but proceeding from a submissive mind. Schleusner's explanation is similar, "Obey your rulers and promptly (or willingly) obey them."(38)

20. The Vulgate Beza and almost all expounders, render it as an imperative, "Know ye."(39)

Printed in Great Britain
by Amazon

78204140R00149